The Glories of an Earth Bound Goddess

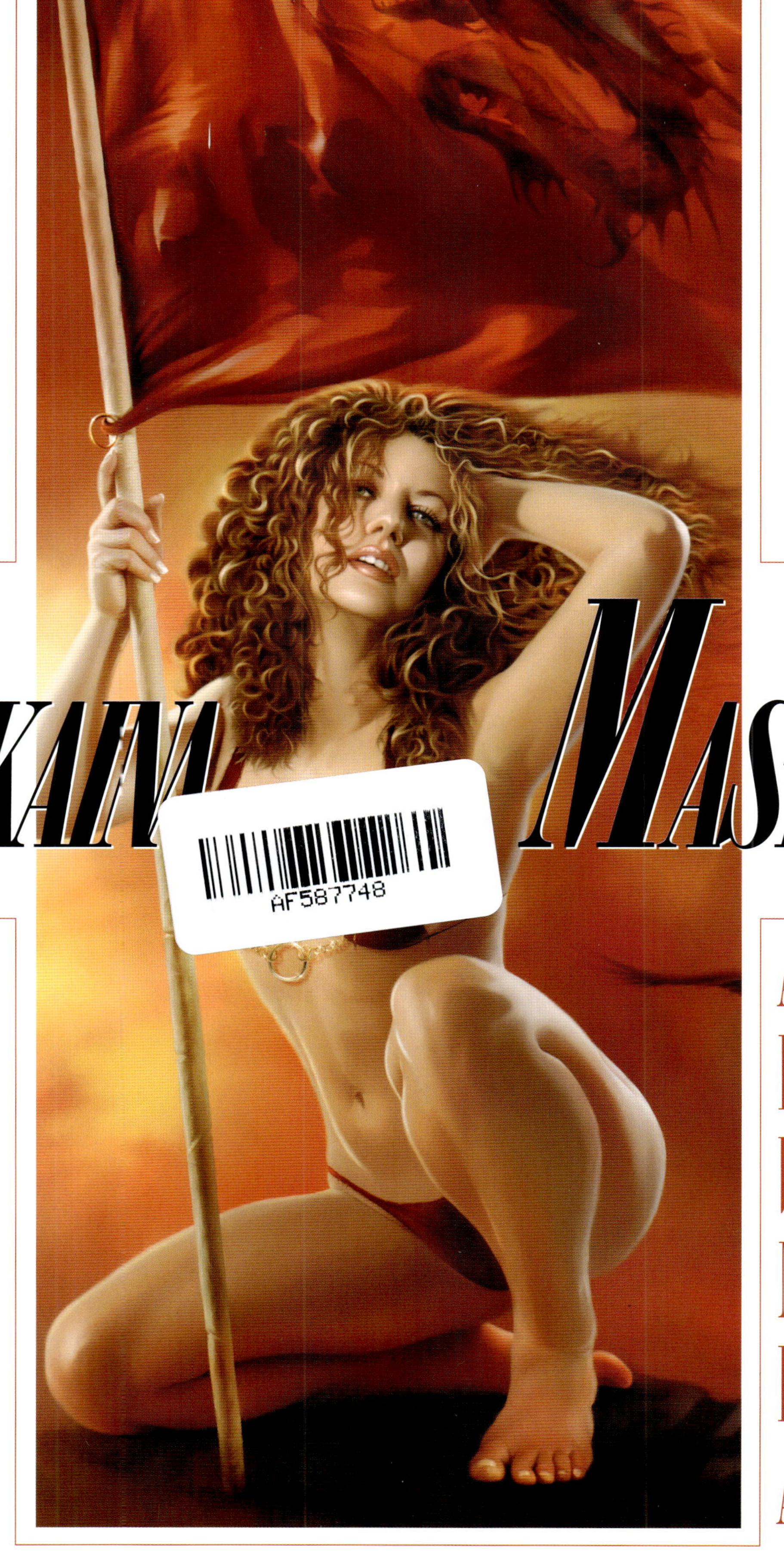

DRAKAINA MASTERS

As Illustrated by Her Most Devoted Admirers

AN SQP PRESENTATION

Are you ready for this?
Are you ready for Drakaina?

Many women are models but only a few become Muses.
Drakaina is one of those women.

You are about to experience something special.
What you hold in your hands is more than a collection of fantastic fantasy art.
It's an invitation from Drakaina to attend the secret and sacred relationship that she has with her artists. It's a celebration of her body, her spirit, her sexuality.
And now, she invites you to experience her in this intimate way as well.

She stands before you nude. In paint, in pencil and in photographs. She wants you to examine her, like every artist does. She wants you to notice the curve of her breast. The dip of her hip. The texture of her skin. The softness of her lips. The blush of her nipples and the wild curls of her hair. She invites you to look at all these things and more... to experience her thoroughly through the artwork. She wants you to know her ... She wants you to feel her... She wants you to see her.

But be warned! She has a spell about her.
This Muse will haunt your dreams. She will come to you at night while you rest secure in bed. She will slide up against you, take you and hold you in her warm embrace. She will press her perfumed flesh against you, lay her bewitching chest upon yours. You will feel her heartbeat. In a breath, she will whisper your name.

She is the forever Muse.
Free with her body, free with her sexuality, free in spirit and forever more. She will remain free. Free to inspire others who are blessed to lay eyes upon her magnificent form.

So I ask you again.
Are you ready for this?
Are you ready for Drakaina?

Jim Balent
Nov 10 2009
From his home studio.

SPECIAL THANKS from Drakaina

Sal and Bob my darling publishers for their patience and for giving me the artistic freedom to put this book together. Working with you is always such a delightful experience. Ariock for his undying support and for allowing me to grow and fly on my own. My fans, for showering me with love since my early days in 2001. And of course all of the artists who chose me as their Muse.

Drakaina - Masters

ISBN 978-0-86562-210-4 Printed in Hong Kong.
Book design by Grassy Knoll Studios.
Published by SQP Inc. - PO Box 248 - Columbus, NJ 08022
Sal Quartuccio & Bob Keenan - Publishers

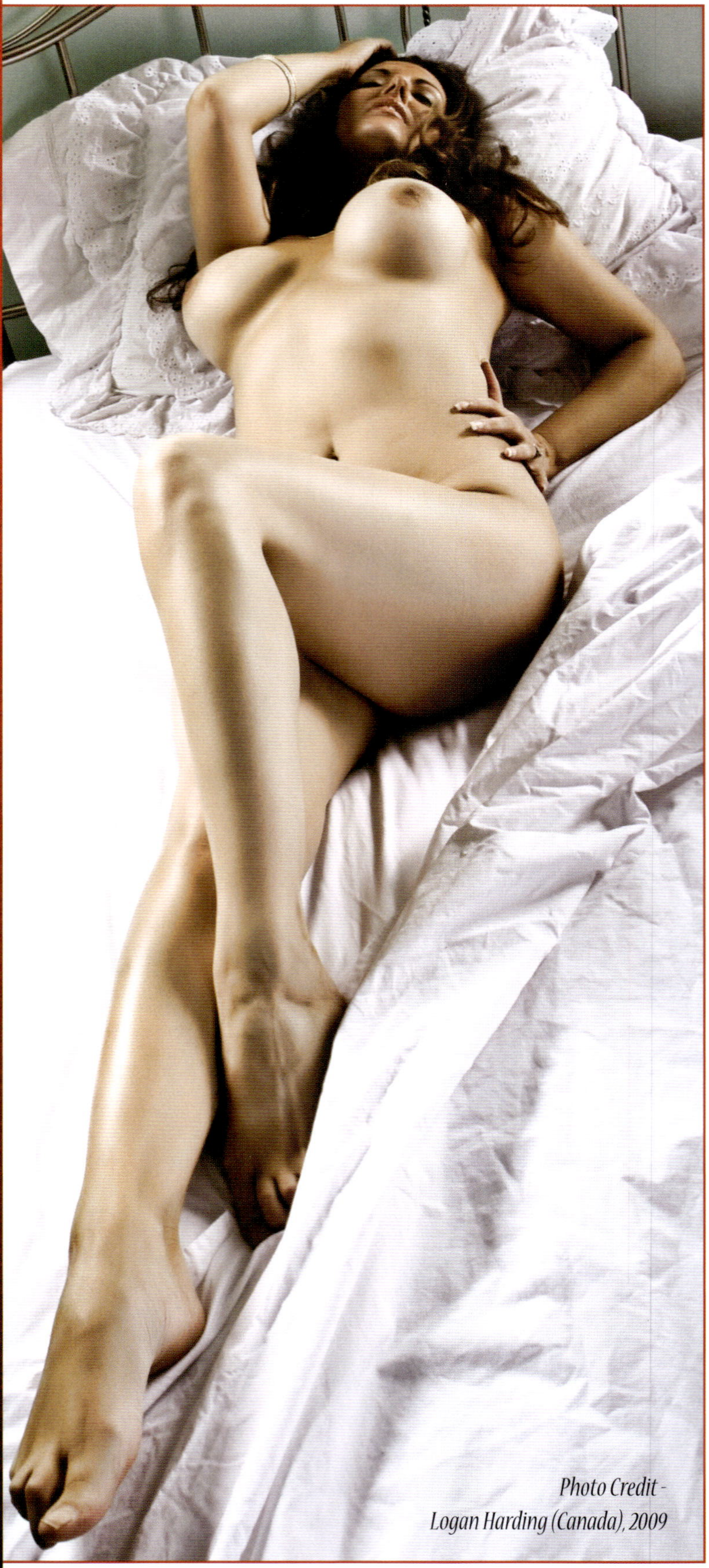

Photo Credit - Logan Harding (Canada), 2009

DRAKAINA MASTERS

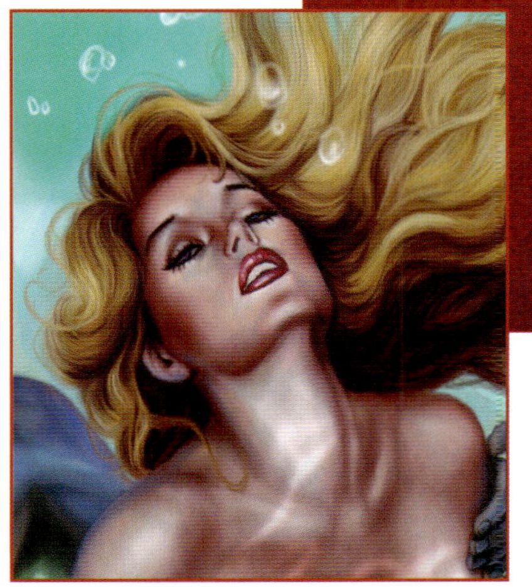

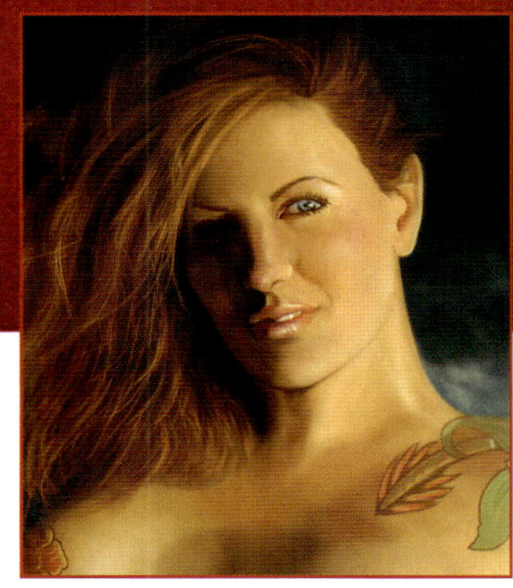

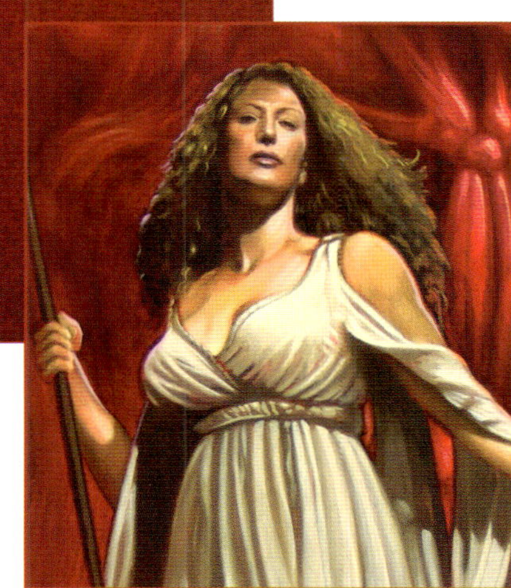

"Because, after all, we are all famous somewhere yet complete strangers to other industries... "

This was the starting point of the Masters art book. Over the past few years, I've had opportunity to work with many incredible fantasy, erotic, comic and pin-up artists, as well as those working as mangakas, and as video game and movie concept designers. What I found so surprising was, outside of their fields of expertise, most of these artists where completely unknown to the public. I decided to bring them all together around one subject, and to do so by posting an open casting call for Drakaina art submissions. This "casting call" gave me the wonderful opportunity to team up with artists from all over (Japan, Thailand, Europe, North and South America) and through this book give them the exposure I believe they richly deserve.

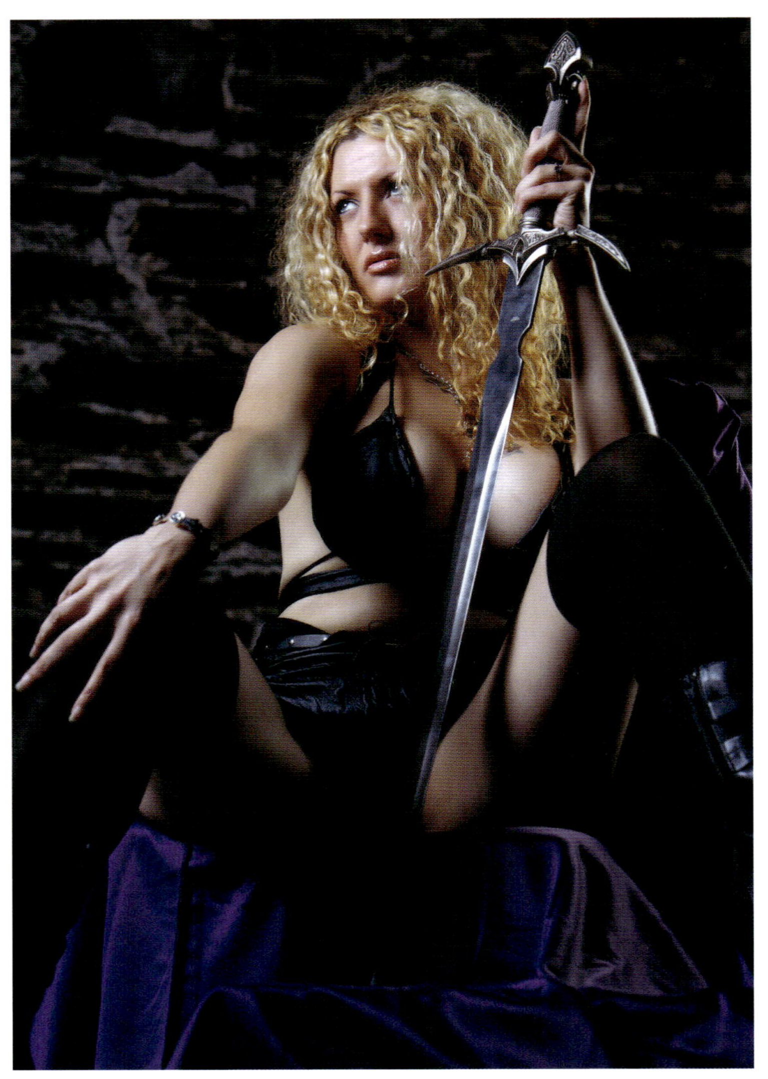

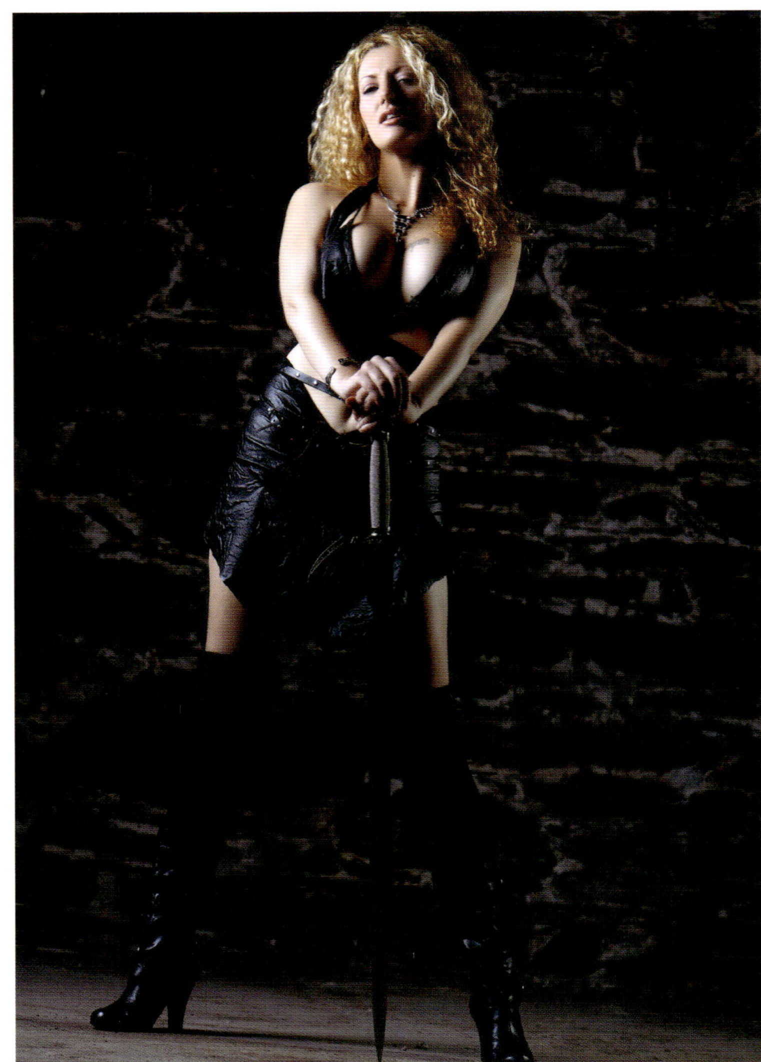

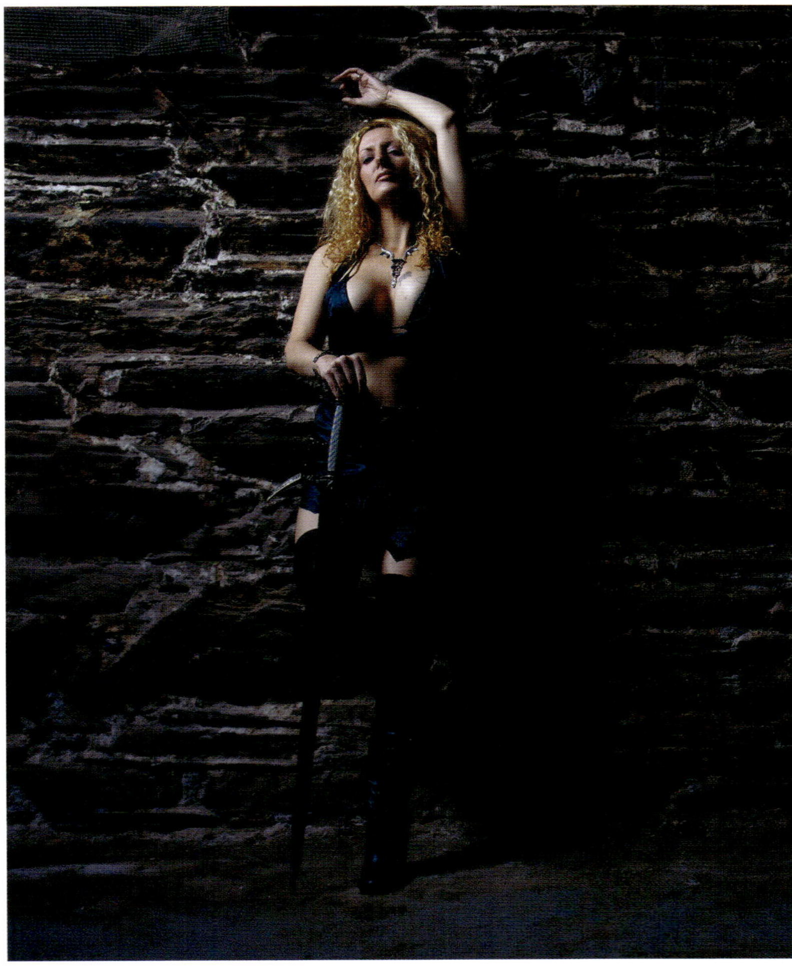

The first 100% fantasy art shoot I did since moving to Canada with a photographer other than Ariock.
And also the first time I got to shoot with Brian, whom I had met at my book launch, which he was covering.
I couldn't be happier with the results...
I mean, photography is a little like sex in the sense that the first try is usually not as good as it could be but this one was an exception: Brian nailed it right away...
From his lights to the angles, to the location he chose, everything was perfect...
The comic book commissioning the pics was absolutely delighted too , so it all worked out beautifully.

Brian Larter is a Halifax based photographer specializing in commercial, science fiction and fantasy subjects.

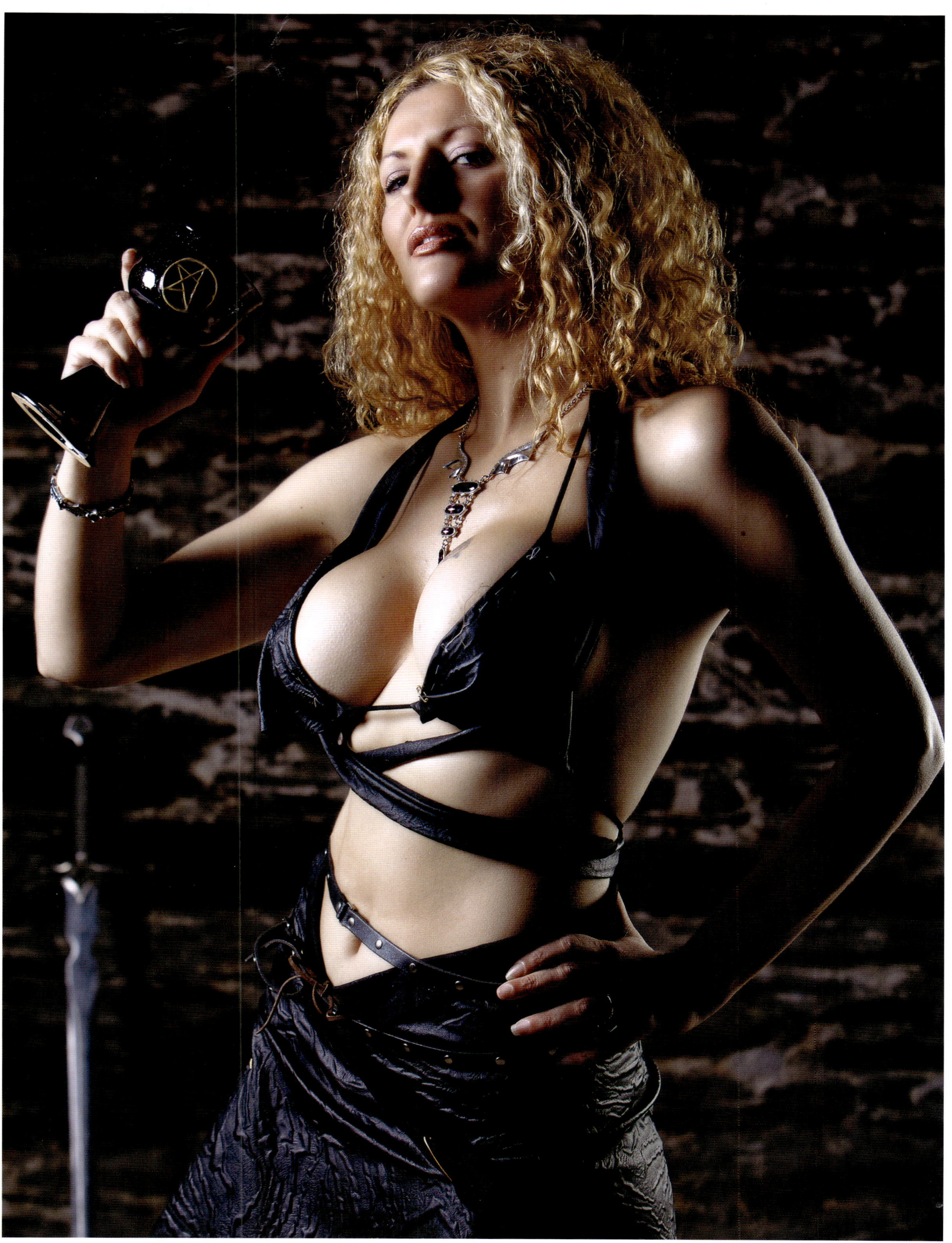

BRIAN LARTER (CANADA), 2009
"The Muse"

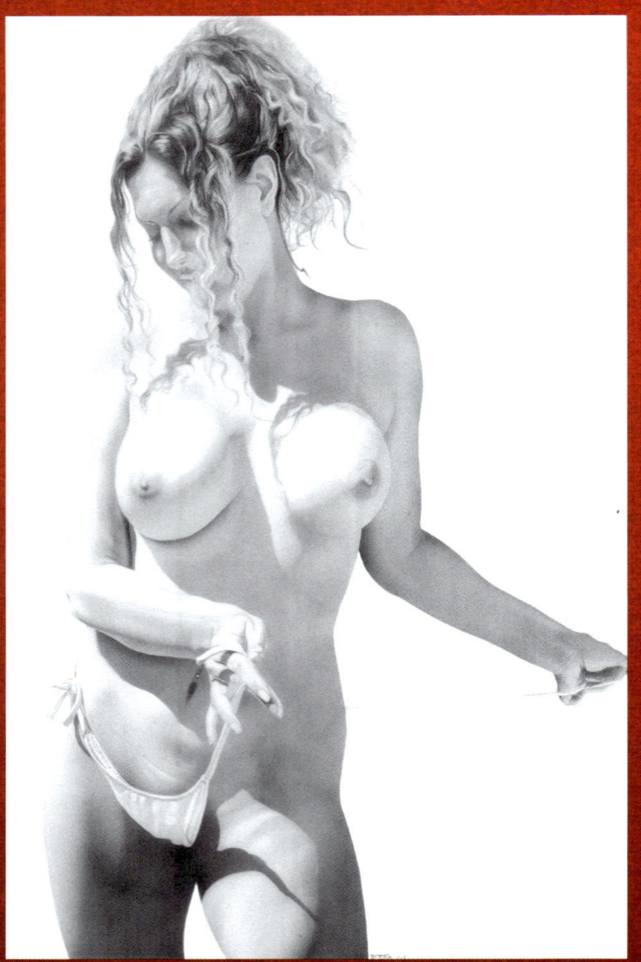

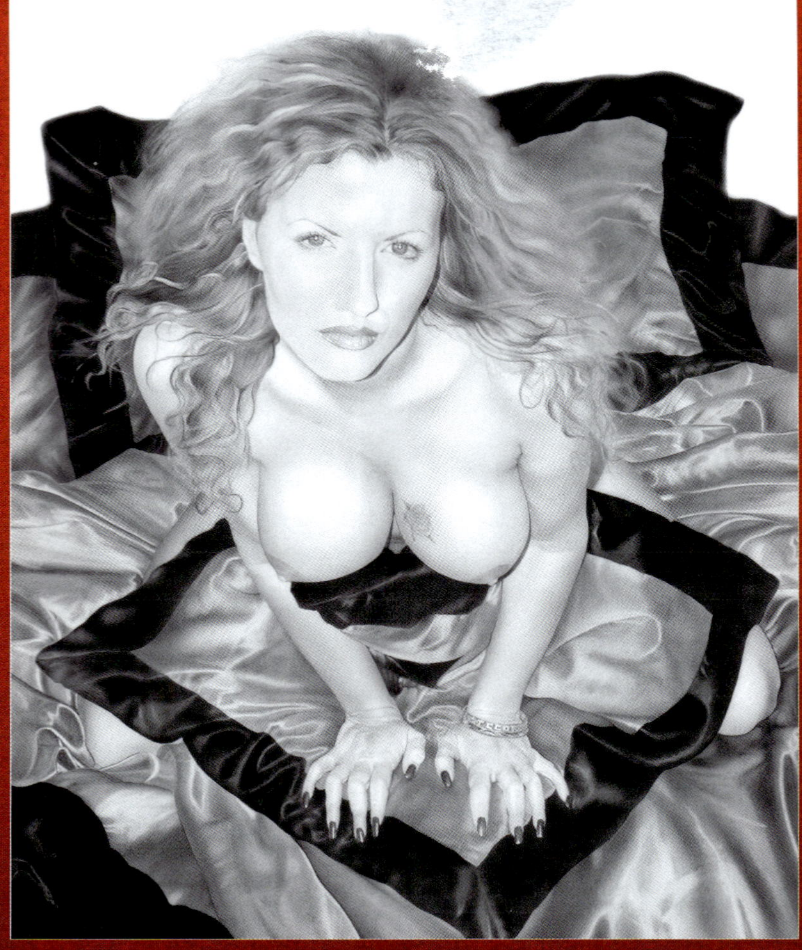

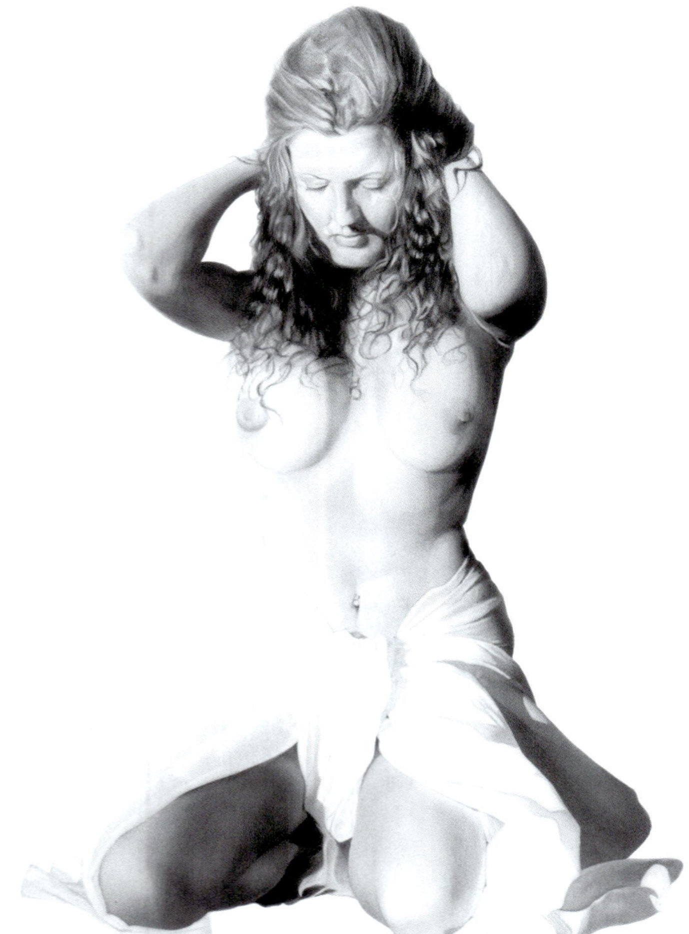

On these 2 pages are some gorgeous examples of black and white artworks. Both Daniel and T.C. have mastered the art of expressing emotions through graphite, making them almost life like...

This page:
T.C.CORR (USA), 2009
"Drakaina"

Opposite page:
DANIEL KIESSLER, (Germany) 2009,
"Pure"

I chose this pose as inspiration for my drawing because I like the pureness and the vibe that Drakaina brings to this picture. This is also emphasized by the lighting and the clothes she wears. It reminds me of some works by the classic traditional artists of the fine arts -- the Masters.

Daniel Kiessler has been working as a freelance artist and erotic fine art illustrator for the international comic industry for 12 years. The beauty of the female form has become his main theme. His artbook "The Art of Daniel Kiessler" was released in 2009 by SQP.

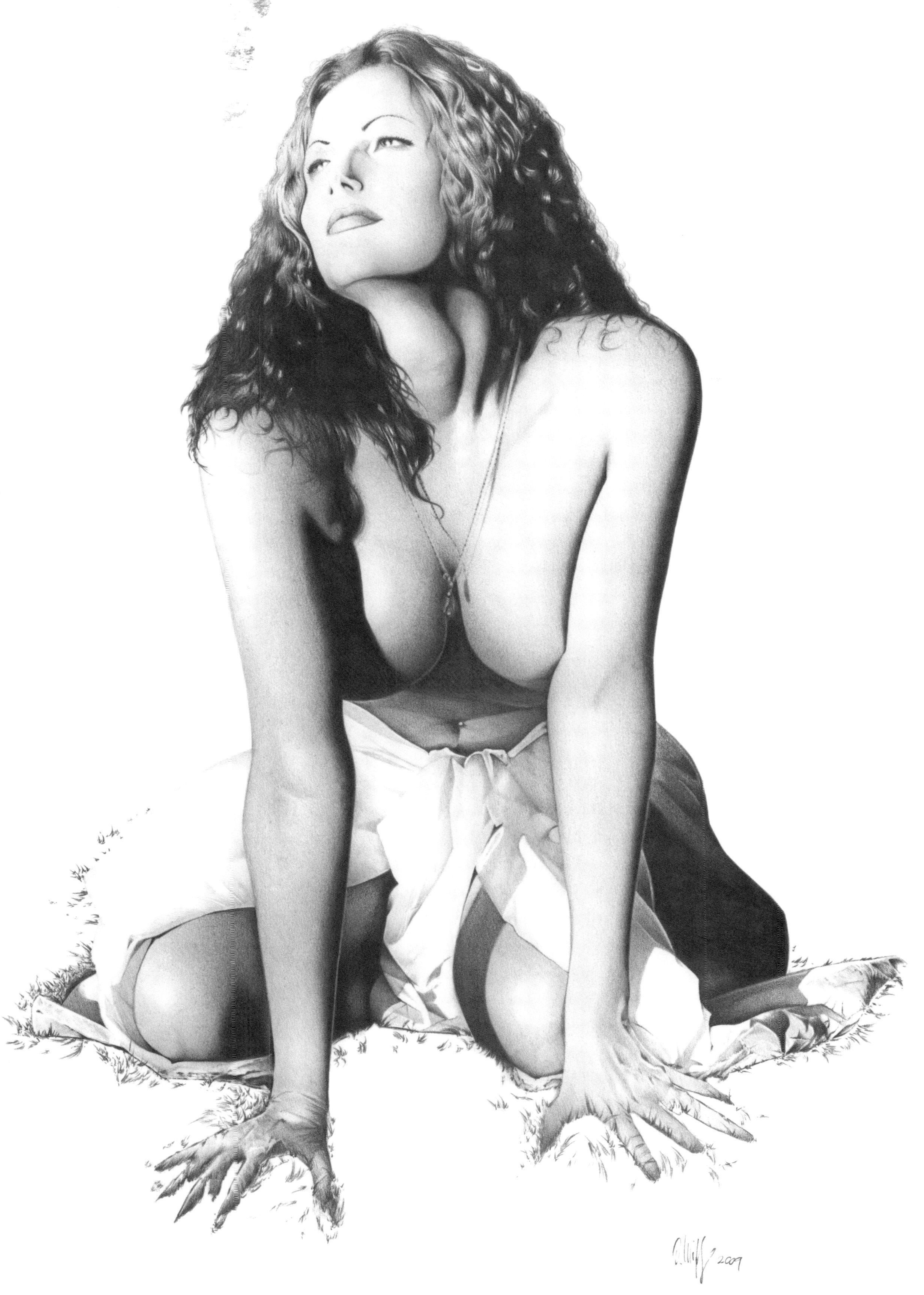
2007

MARCO GUAGLIONE (ITALY), 2009
"Eye Candy Poker"

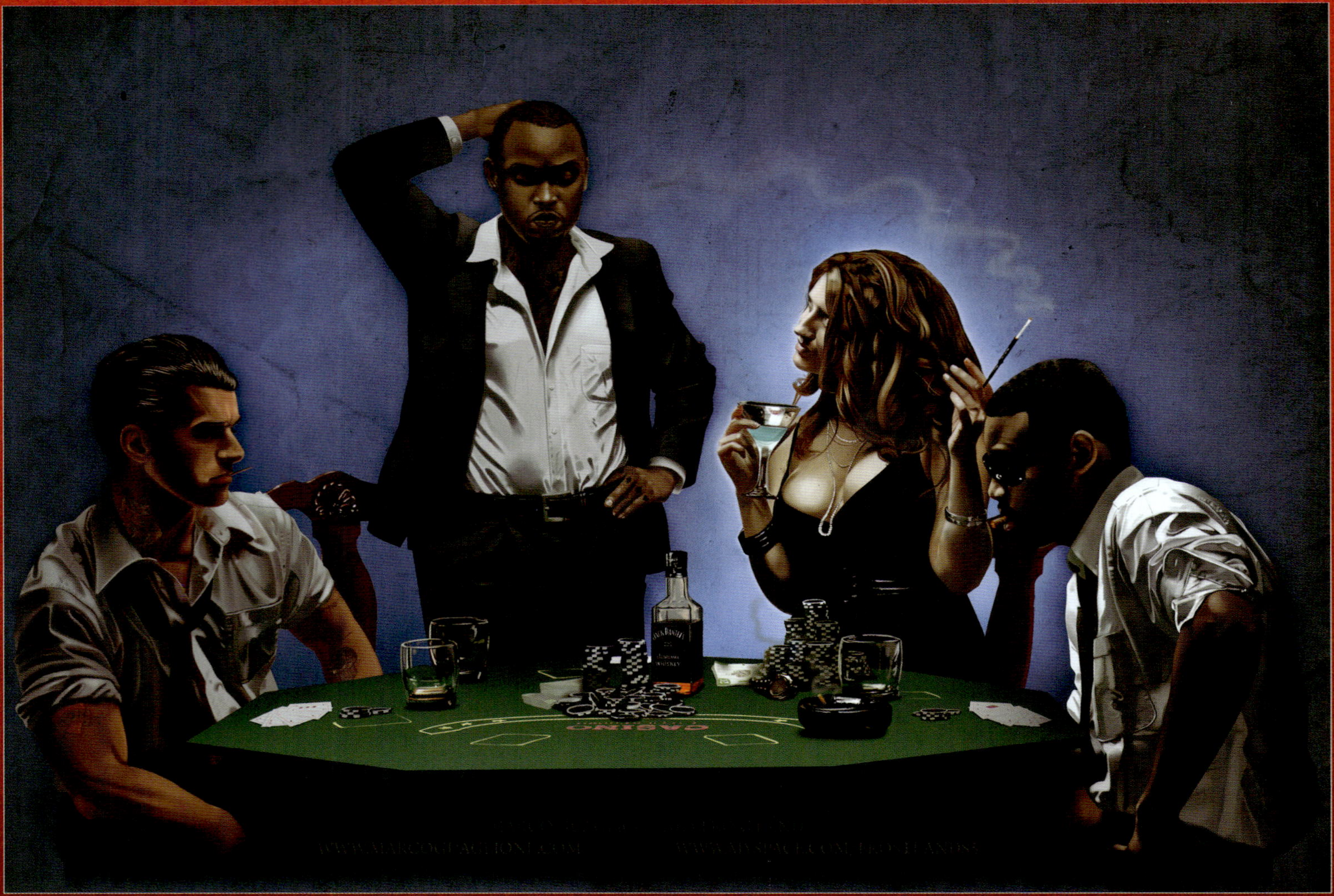

Marco Guaglione is an Italian pin-up artist who has been drawing since his early years. Super heroes and comic books characters were his great passion and he spent more time drawing than listening to classes (where he learned that school desks could be a great canvas for his art).
Then Marco discovered pin-up art through the art of Gil Elvgren and soon after digital art.
Ever since he has been painting pin-ups, collaborating with famous pin-up models and actresses, while doing private commissions for both commercial and private clients.

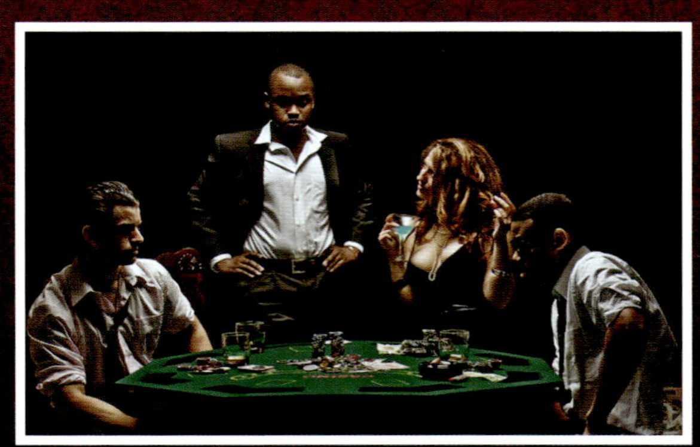

NICK RUDNICKI (CANADA), 2009
"Drakaina Poker Face"

This is one of my favorite pictures for a photoshoot that was commissioned by an European Poker Magazine, and in which I had the pleasure to pose with three dear friends, whom only one was an actual model. The thing is, for this shoot I needed three real poker players and was unable to find three male models that were both sexy & played poker. I turned to my friends, whom I knew really enjoyed playing poker and, why deny it, were really kind to the eye.
The "Gangsta meets Hollywood" feel of the shoot is a combination of my vision of the shoot, Nick's incredible skills and the overall energy of every one involved. Definitely one of my fave non fantasy related shoots of 2009. I was really pleased when Marco was inspired by it for his artwork.
Nick Rudnicki is a commercial and fashion photographer based in Halifax, Nova Scotia.

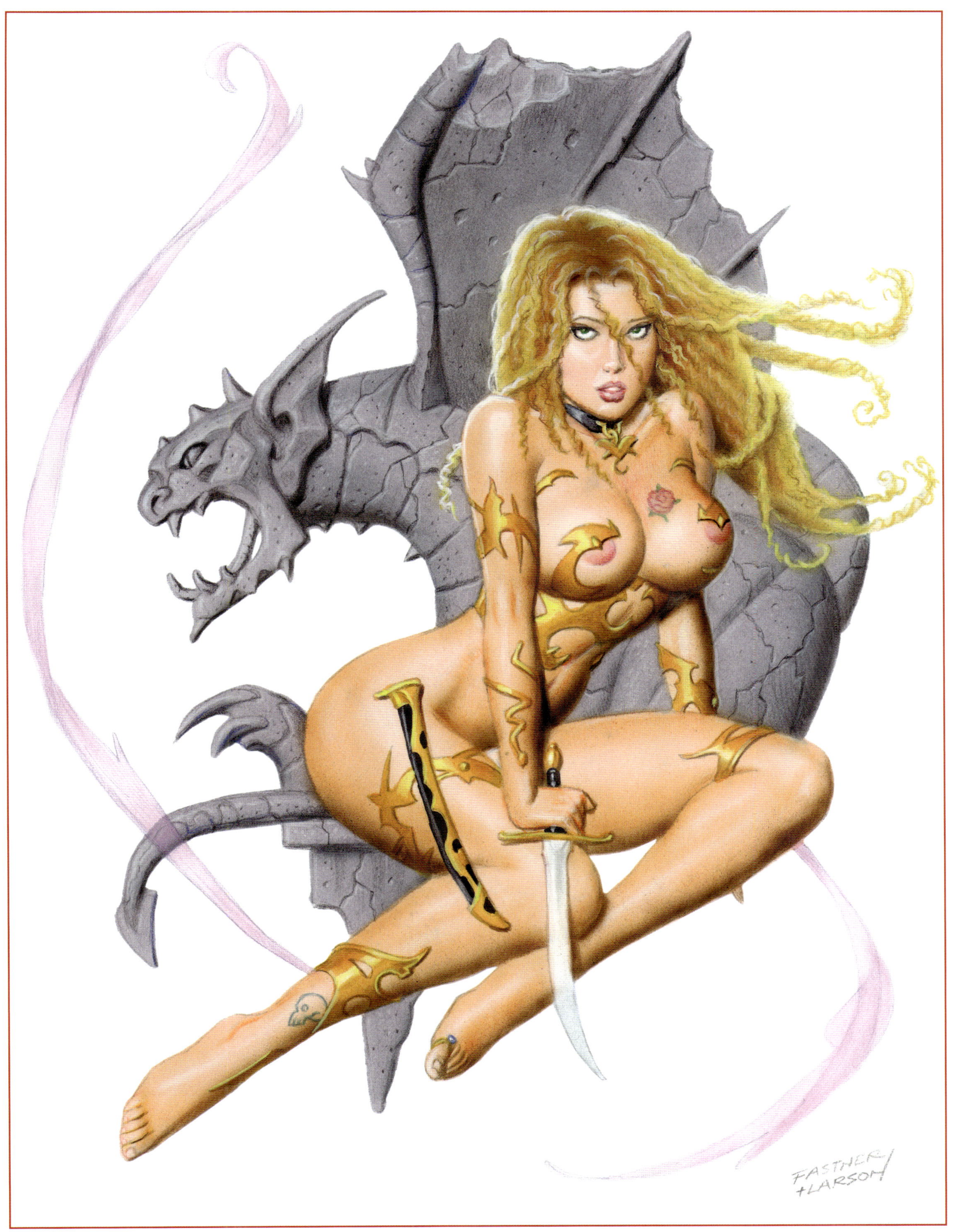

FASTNER & LARSON (USA), 2009

As they describe their process so well on their website, F&L constitute an airbrush artist (Steve Fastner), a penciller (Rich Larson), and a crazy dream (mostly involving lusty wenches in and out of strange situations and their clothing ...) and it's been going on for the past 28 years.

TCHAL (FRANCE), 2009

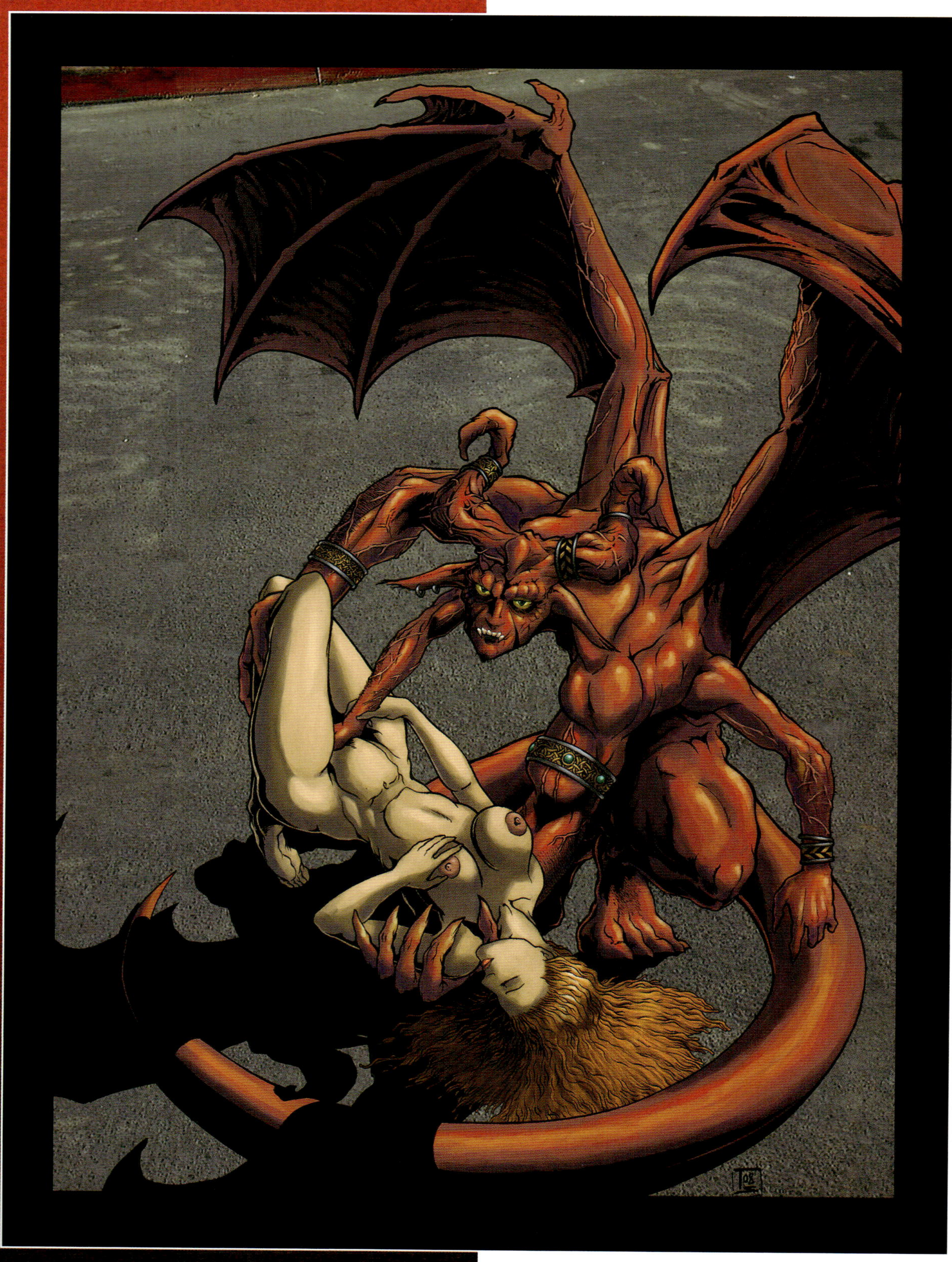

"Pornography"
I wanted to draw a monster that day.
The idea of this monster having sex, without any feeling, with Drakaina, who had become a mere sexual object. The monster looking at you, the reader, it's accomplice.

Opposite page
ONEQ (JAPAN), 2009
"The Goddess of Thunder" (Nyoraijin)
There is a God called 'RAIJIN' in Japan. I drew my inspiration from that deity and the mysterious imagery of Drakaina.

Oneq was born in 1981 in Japan. As a freelance illustrator, she draws a wide range of art, such as wall paintings, flyers, and cartoons which are displayed around the world.

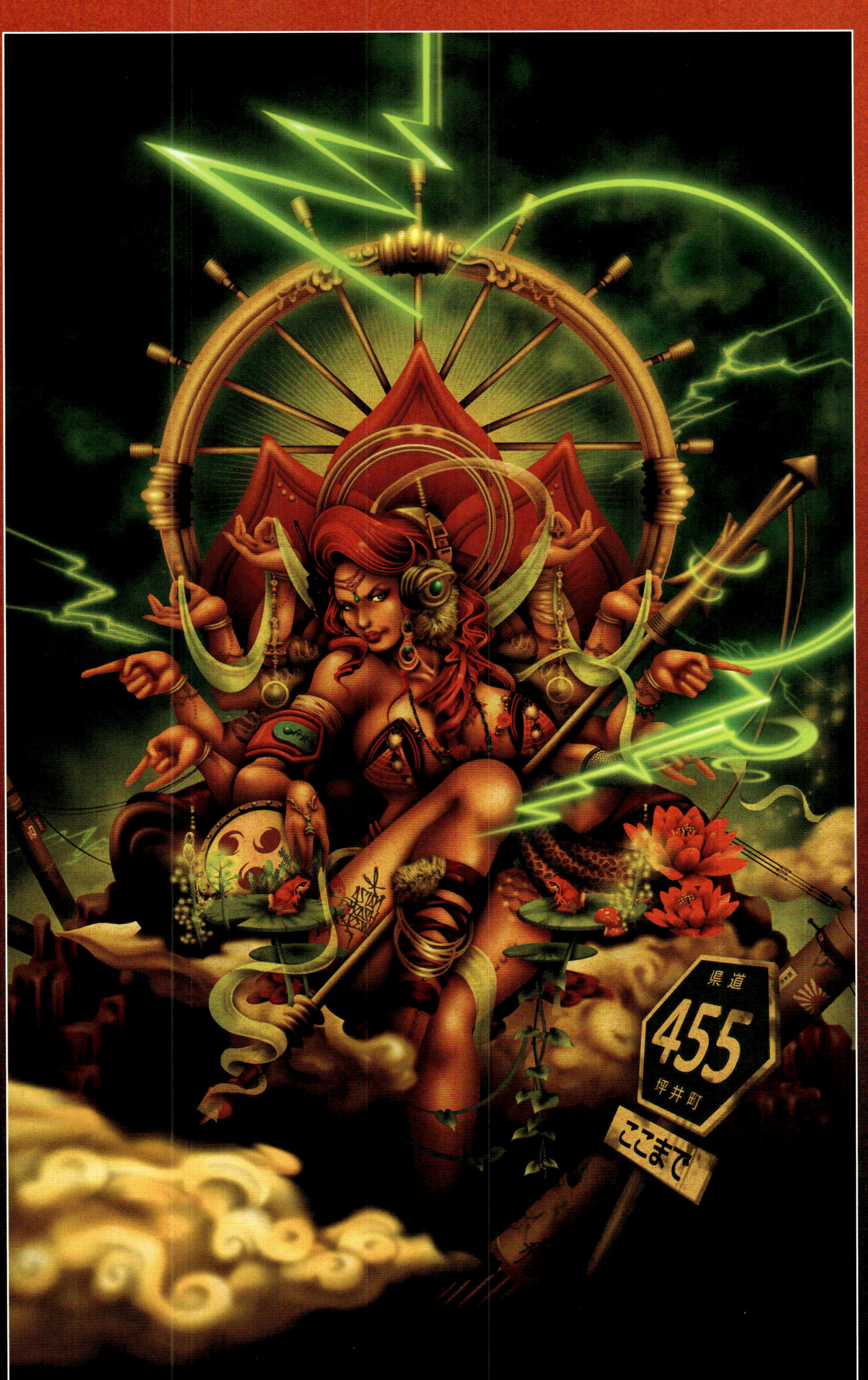
県道
455
坪井町
ここまで

TCHAL & DOLE (FRANCE), 2008

"Dragon Knight"

The first comic book that was given to me was a copy of Olivier Ledroit's "Chroniques de la Lune Noire" and I have been fascinated by dragons ever since.

Tchal lives in the Parisian suburbs where he uses his free time to draw and perfect his techniques.

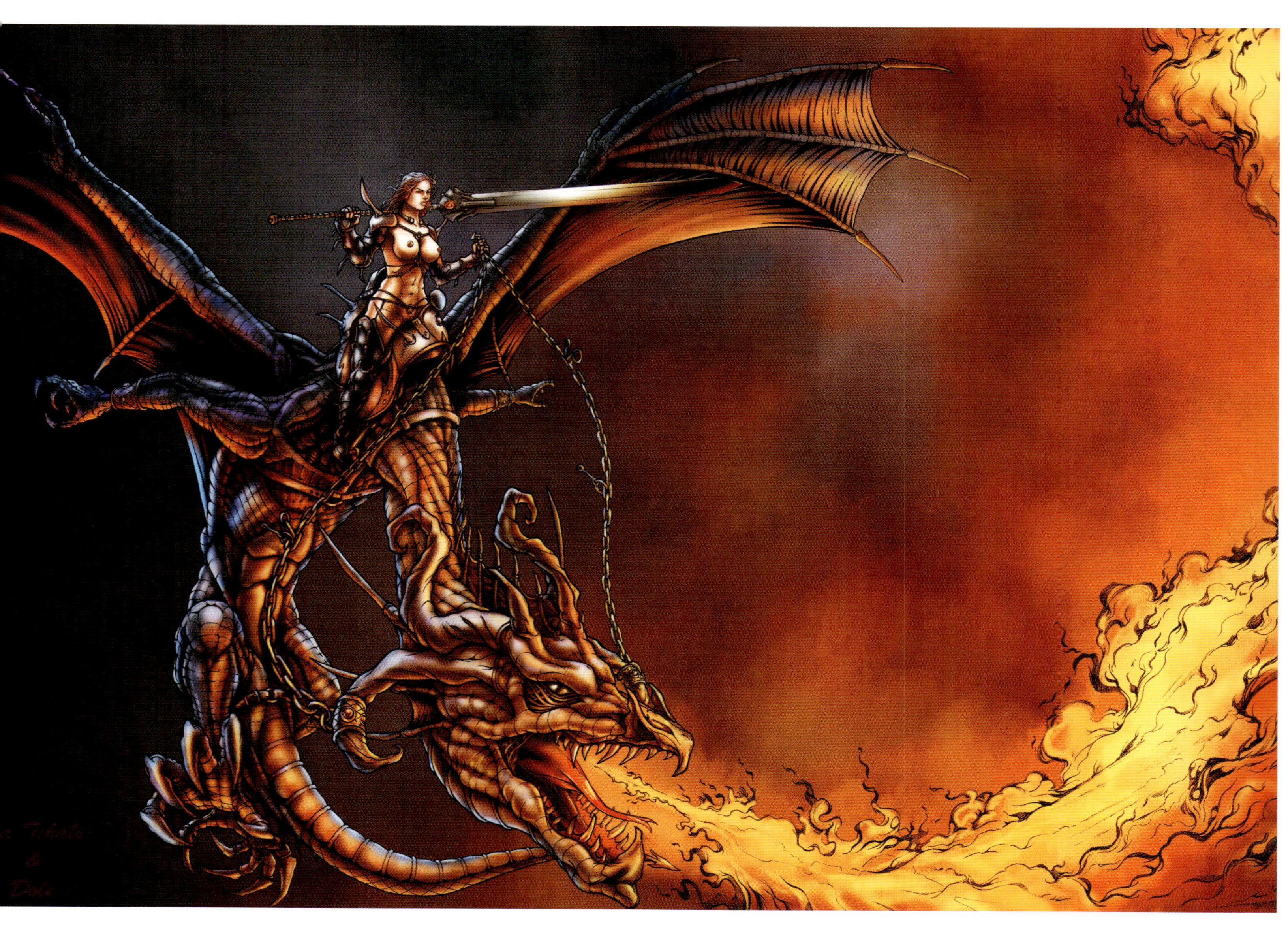

Opposite page:

EDWARD REED (USA), 2009

"Drakaina Dominion"

Drakaina demands your attention! Her arresting beauty, commanding presence and graceful sensuality is everything an artist wants to capture in a fantasy painting! My concept for Drakaina is she has claimed her territory and is making it known that she is ready to defend it!

Edward Reed is a noted authority on pinup art and has written many instructional articles on the subject for a variety of art publications. He is the editorial advisor/contributing editor for ART SCENE INTERNATIONAL magazine and his artbooks are published by SQP.

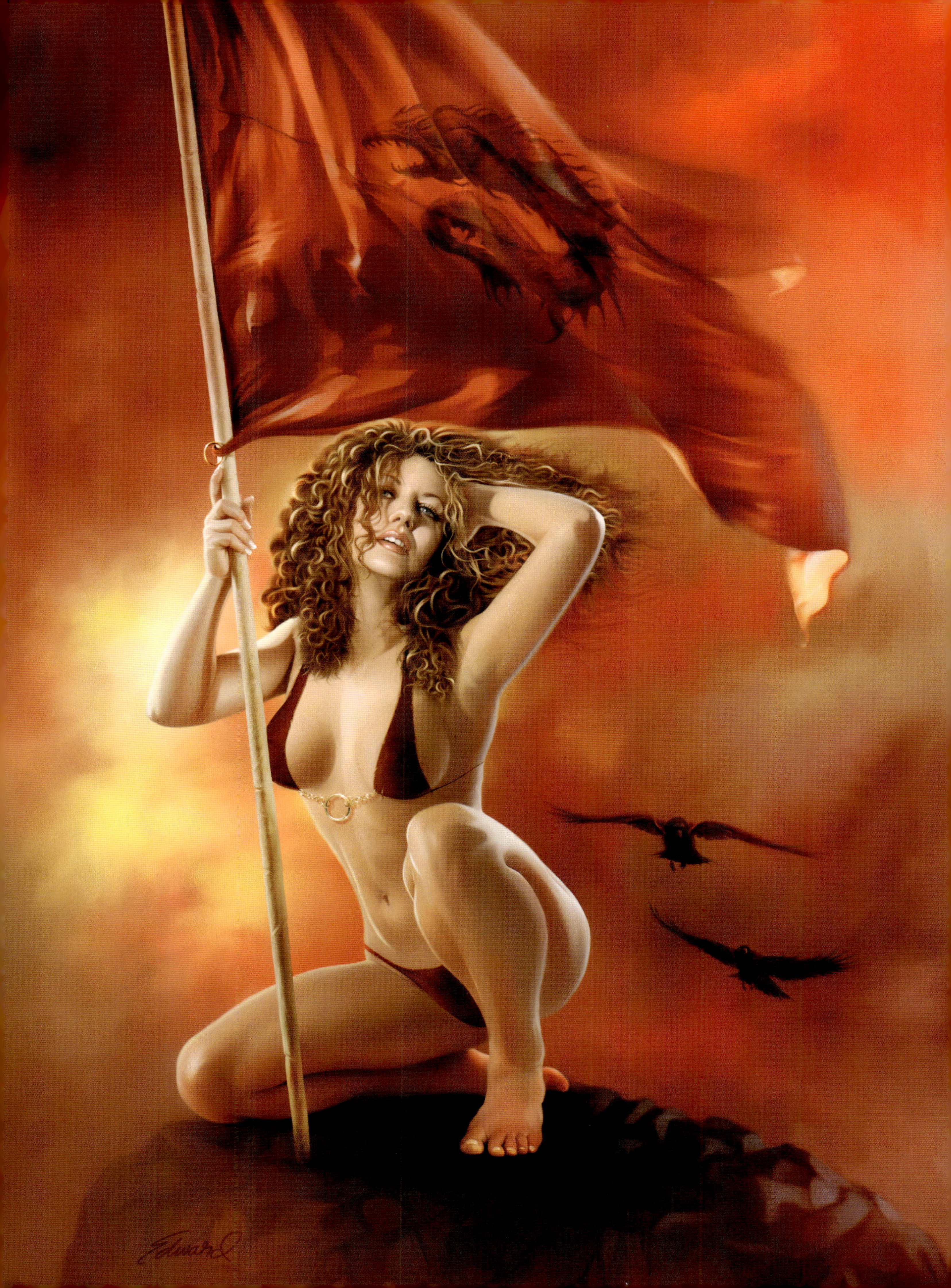
Edward

UWE JARLING

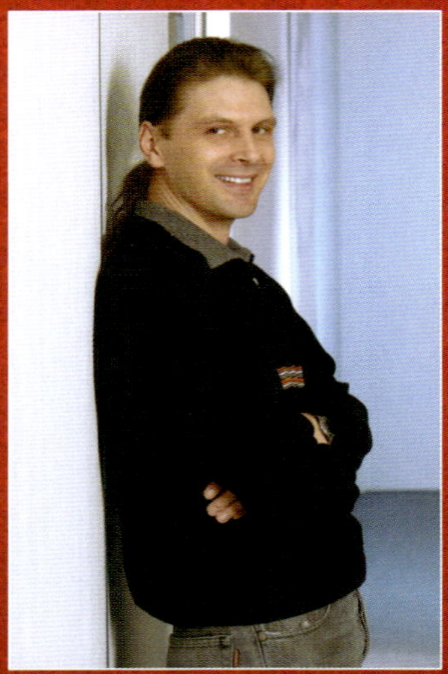

MASTERS WINNER

Choosing a winner for the Masters competition was not an easy task. We received many beautiful artworks oozing with talent and creativity.Yet, Uwe's artwork really stood out, appealing both to male and female members of the jury.

UWE JARLING was born in 1968. After graduating with a degree in graphic design he worked as an illustrator and graphic designer. His first work consisted of covers for videos and books as well as technical and architectural illustrations for advertising agencies. An important step in his development followed in 2000 when Uwe started to develop his "fantasy artwork" more seriously and did his first attempts creating art on a computer.

Some of his clients in the fantasy illustration field include Moonstone Books, Bastei, Random House, Fantasy Flight Games, North East Games, MIB, Madison Video, Elfra Filmproduktion, Movie Media, Gameforge AG, Metal Blade Records, Slaney Records, Occupa GmbH, Virgin Lands, 13 Mann Verlag, Spiral Direct, to name a few.

He also done graphic design for clients like Beiersdorf, CISCO, Coty Deutschland, Deutsche Post AG, Gabotex, Golden Lady, HawaiianTropic, Johnson & Johnson, Krüger GmbH & Co. KG, L'Oréal, Mapa GmbH, Procter & Gamble, Sara Lee, Tradepoint, Unilever etc.

A word from the artist "Many people ask me how I can do so many fantasy paintings while I work in the advertising industry all day, well that's simple to answer. By day I'm the well-behaved graphic designer, by night I turn into this crazy illustrator and paint worlds and creatures that no one has ever seen before, it's as simple as that. All you need is the will to work really hard, to learn as much as you can every day and most important – have a real passion for fantasy art.

The next question people often ask me is, why don't you do your fantasy art all day? Well, I love to work with typography as well, so why shouldn't I do both things that I like. Not to mention that I worked as a full time freelance illustrator for about eleven years which was a great time but as a freelancer you always work alone all day, every day. So now I really enjoy working in a team of fabulous colleagues by day and doing my art in the evenings.I might jump back into full time freelancing again some day in the future, but currently I'm happy as it is. I think that's all , hope you enjoy my art as much as I enjoyed doing it!"

Contact info:

Uwe Jarling(Illustrator / Dipl. Grafik-Designer) - E-Mail: uwe@jarling-arts.com - Website: www.jarling-arts.com
Betlinshausener Str.7 89257 Illertissen Germany/Bavaria Telephone: +49 7303 7479 fax: +49 7303 902513

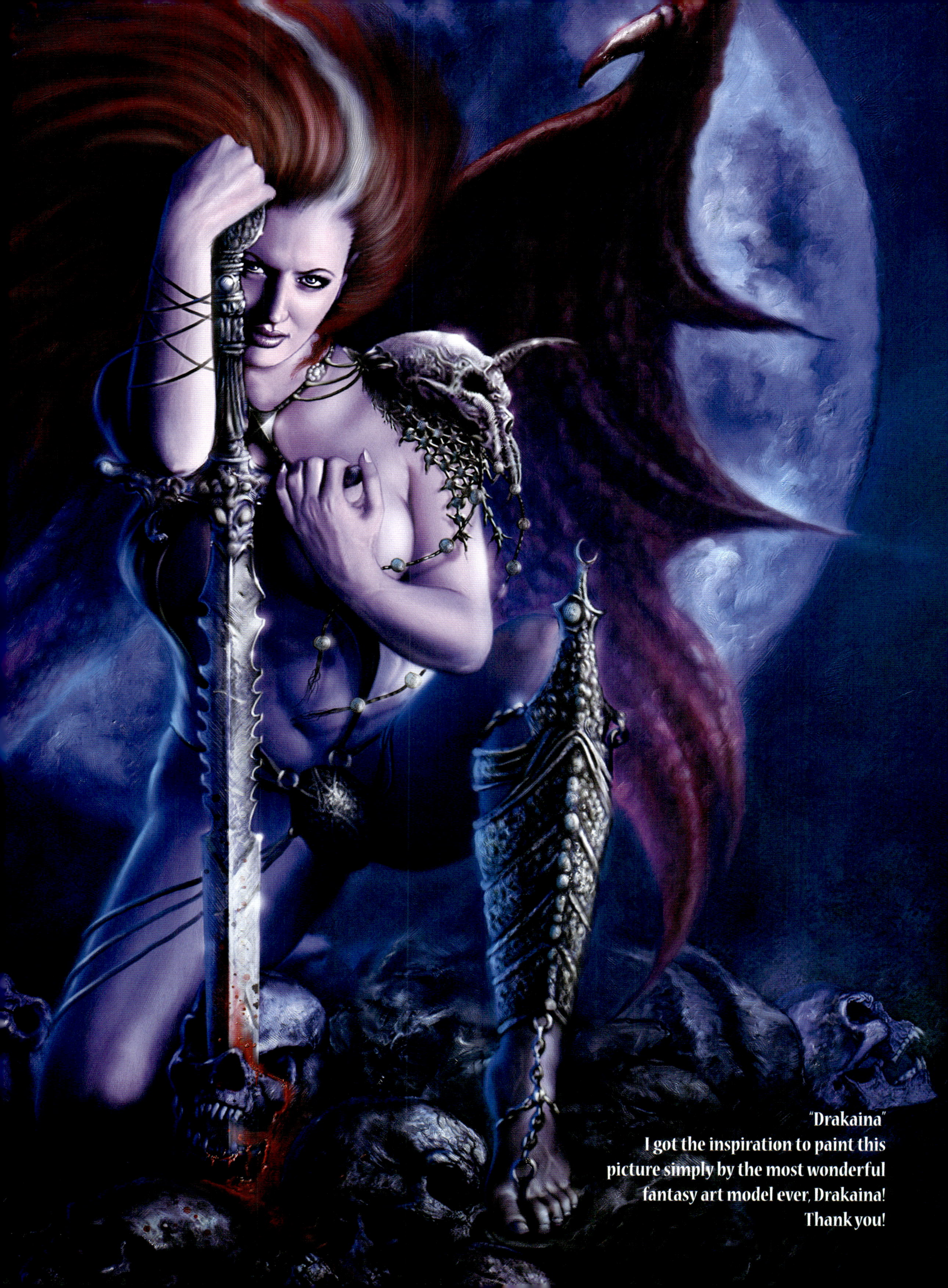

"Drakaina"
I got the inspiration to paint this picture simply by the most wonderful fantasy art model ever, Drakaina! Thank you!

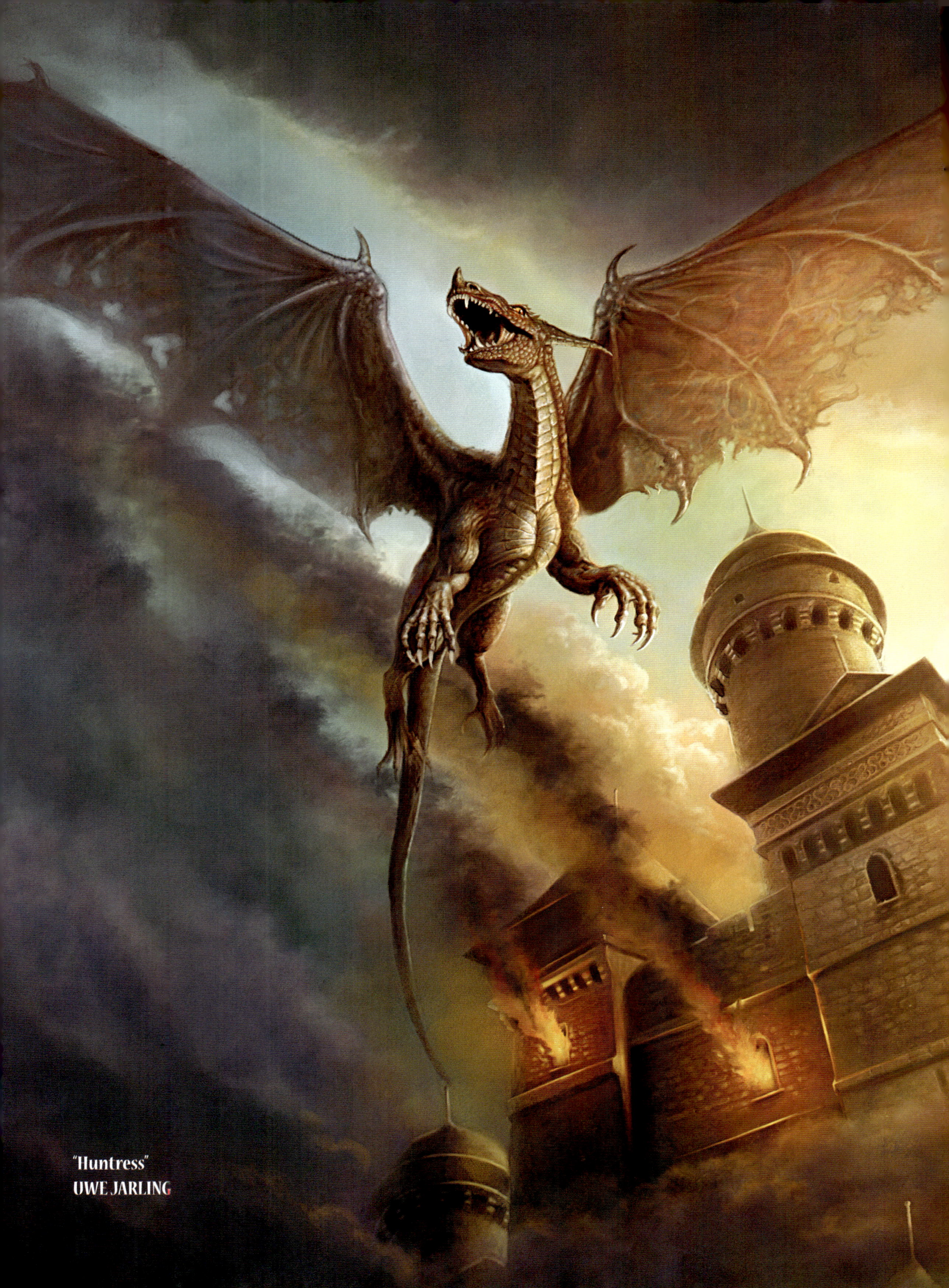

"Huntress"
UWE JARLING

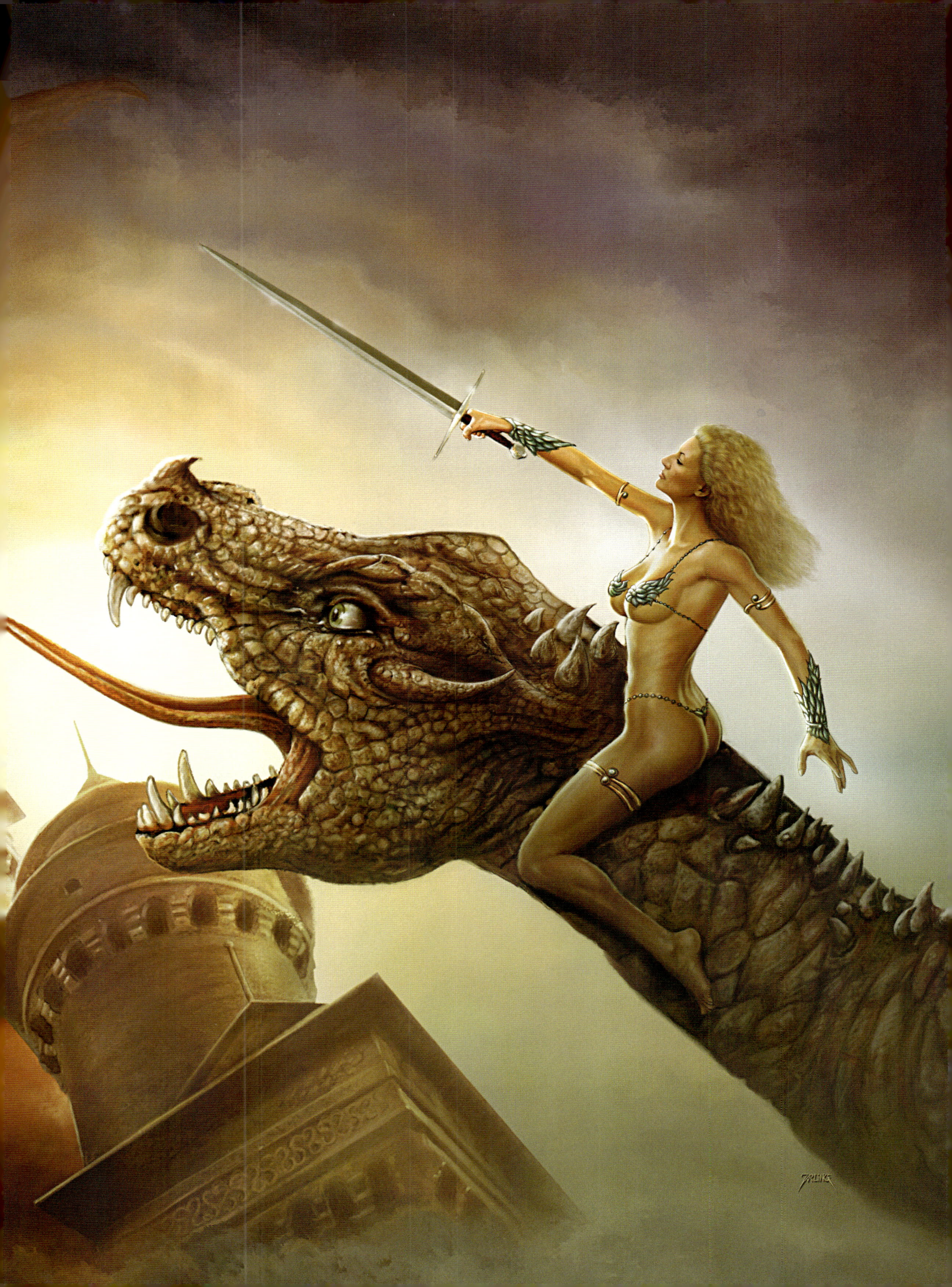

DRAKAINA MASTERS

RUNNERS UP

4 different styles, 4 different techniques and even 4 different countries. But a common level of skills in their own fields, these artists all came very close to the winning title.

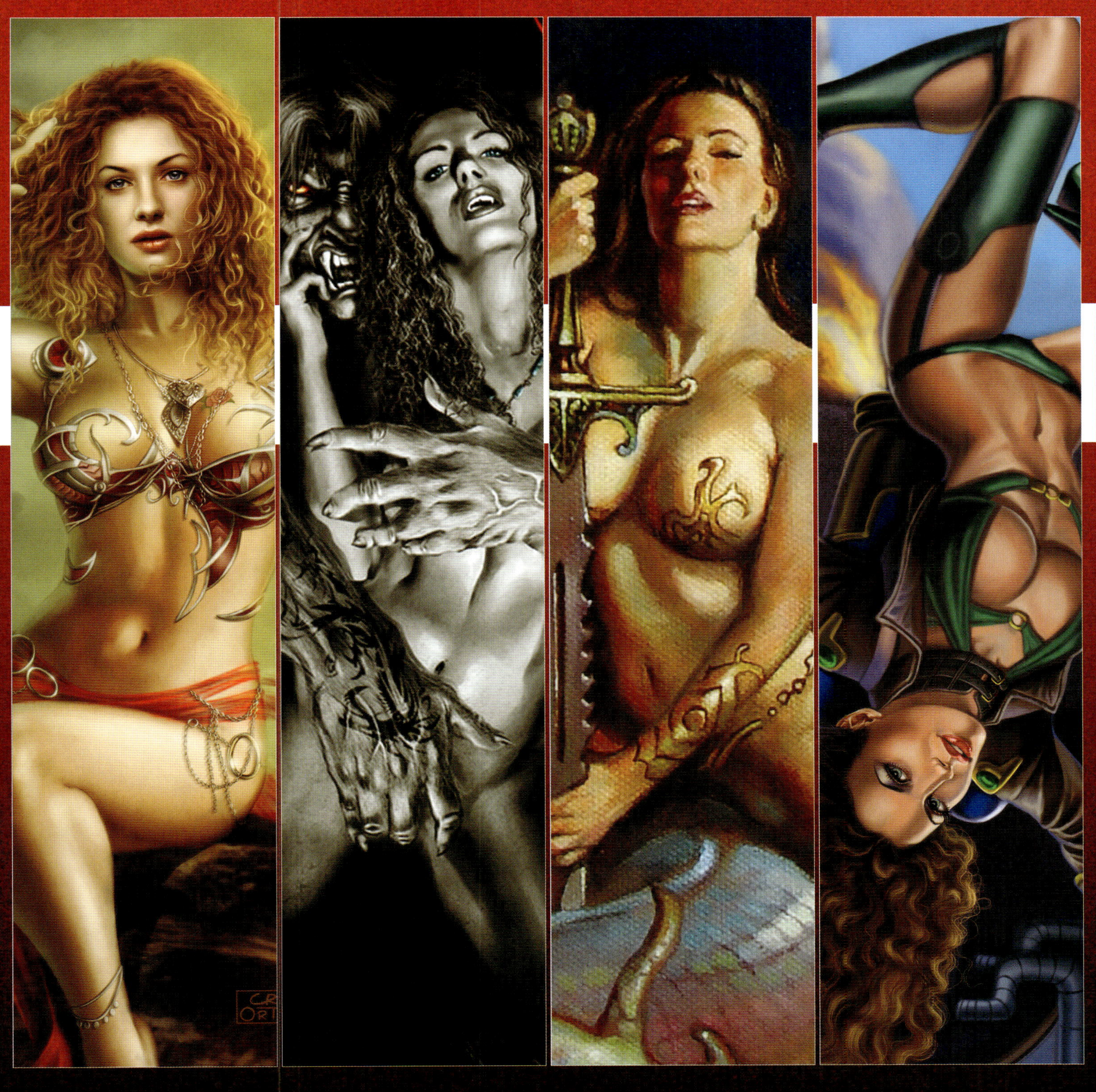

BEST
Technical CG:
Ethereal Warrior by
CRIS ORTEGA

BEST
Gothic Art:
Romeo & Juliet by
BYRON CASTILLO

BEST
Old School Tribute:
Drakaina by
DIDIER NORMAND

BEST
Comic Style Pin-up:
Retro Drakaina by
SANDRA CHANG ADLAIR

CRIS ORTEGA (SPAIN), 2009
"Drakaina"

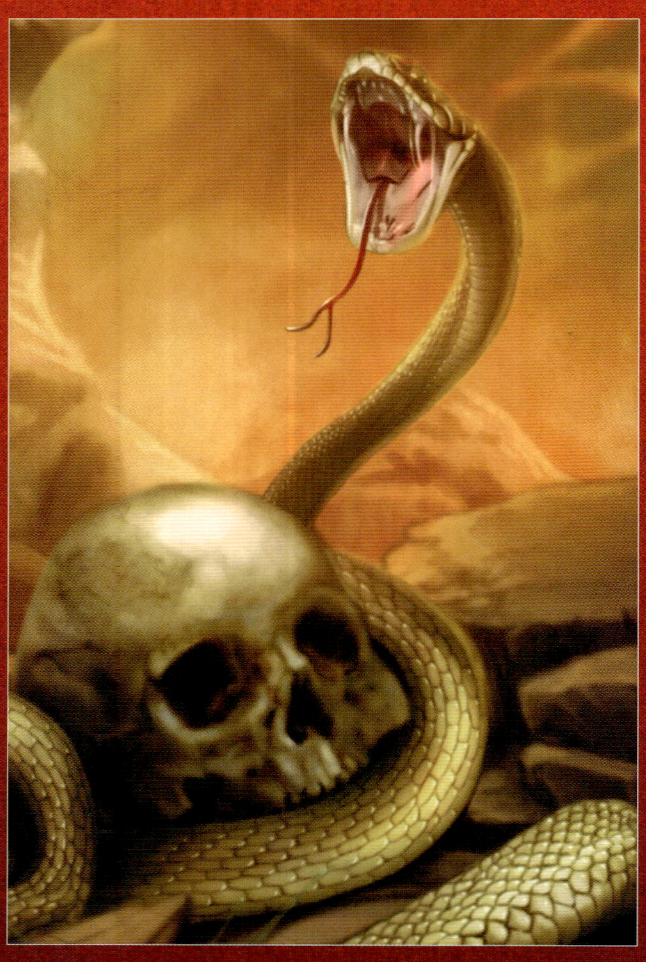

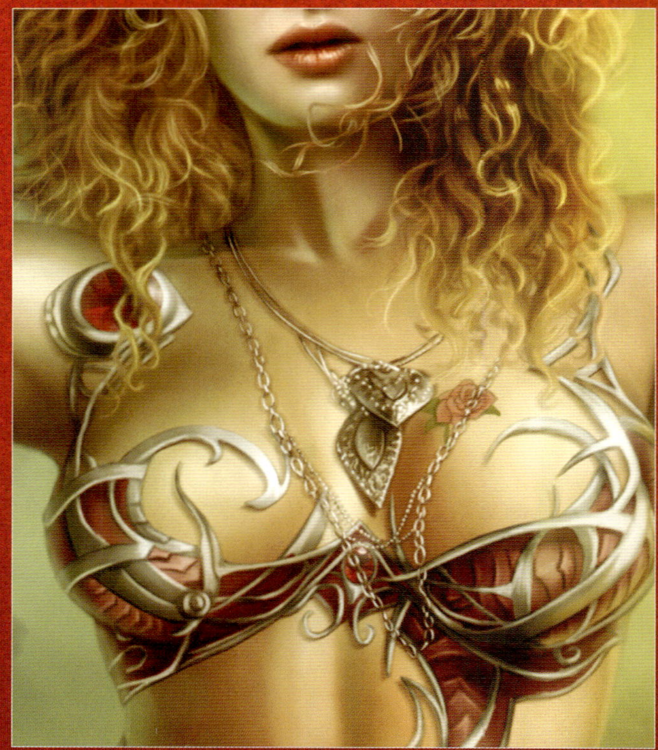

The impressive and extensive artistic and technical skills of Spanish artist Cris Ortega have her working in several fields. Her portfolio includes work from graphic design and advertising to RPG and video games concept design & art, comic books, photography, cover design and logos.

Her most recent works have been published in artbooks like Exotique and Spectrum, as well as on several merchandising products, like jigsaws and posters.

Right now she's working on the third volume of her art book "Forgotten" and on several commission works.

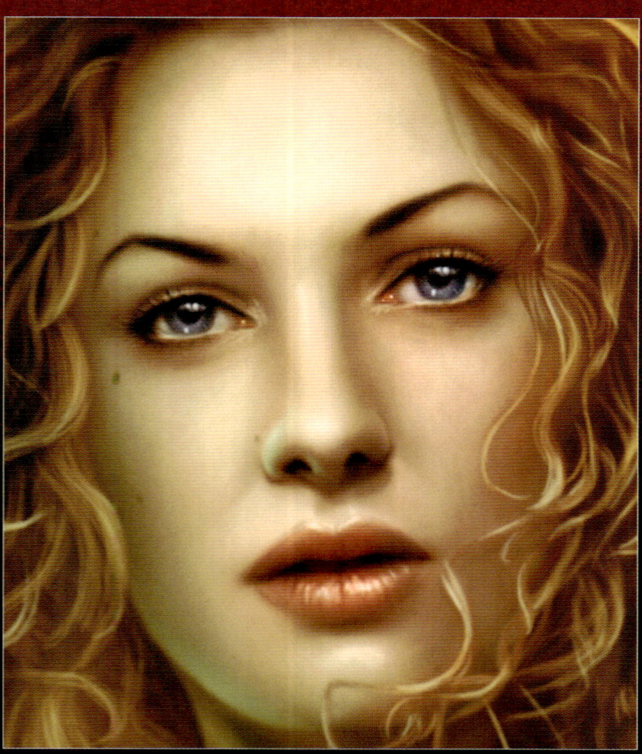

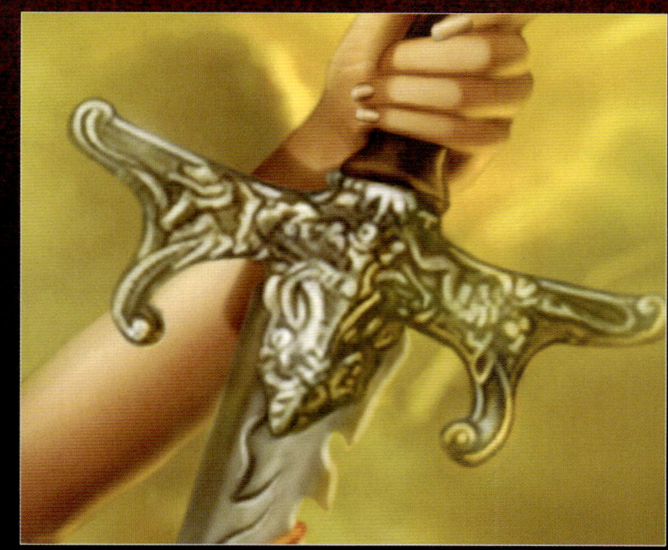

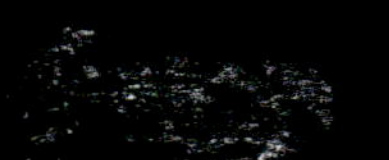

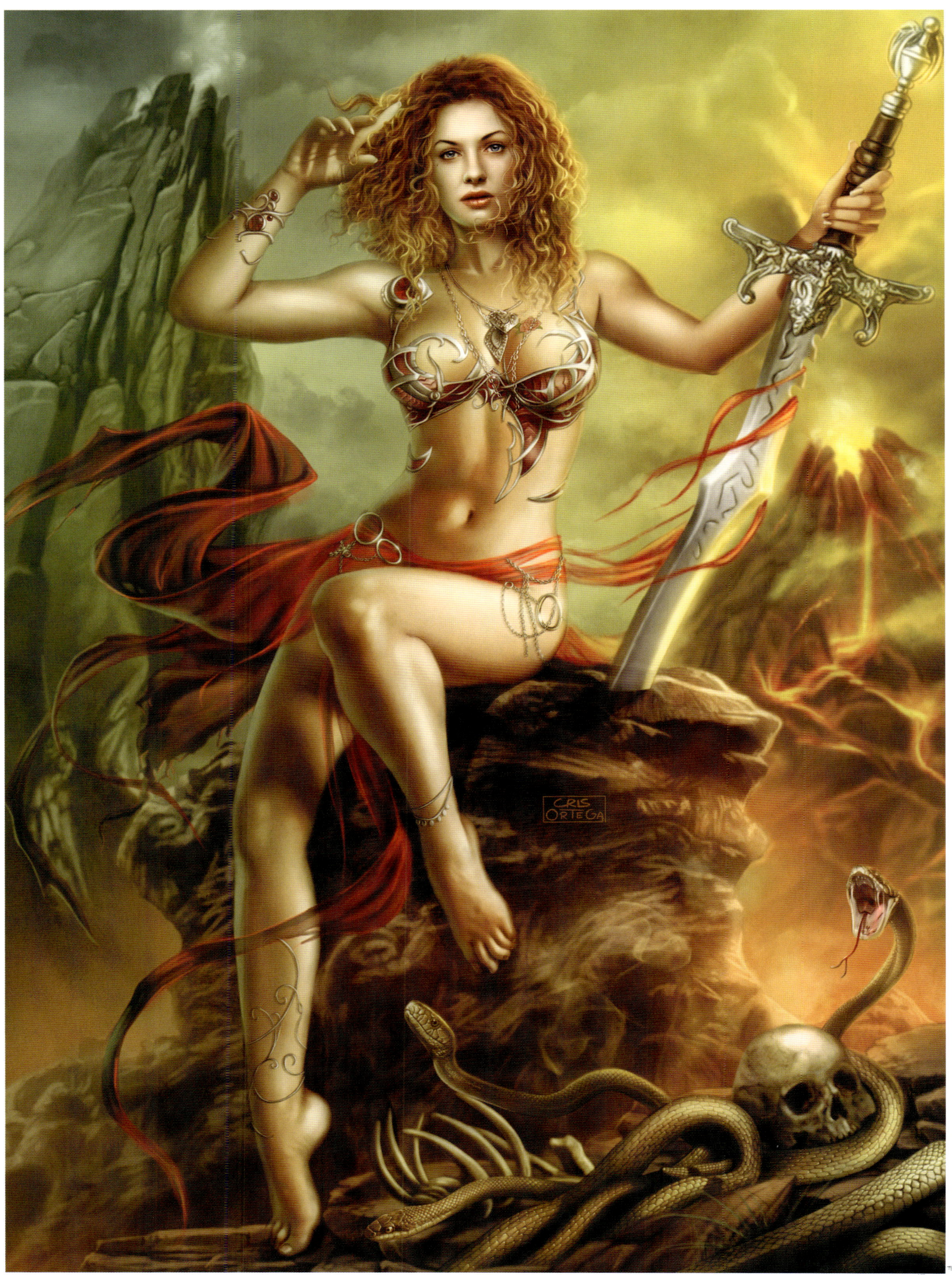
CRIS
ORTEGA

DIDIER NORMAND (France), 2009
Drakaina Dragon Slayer

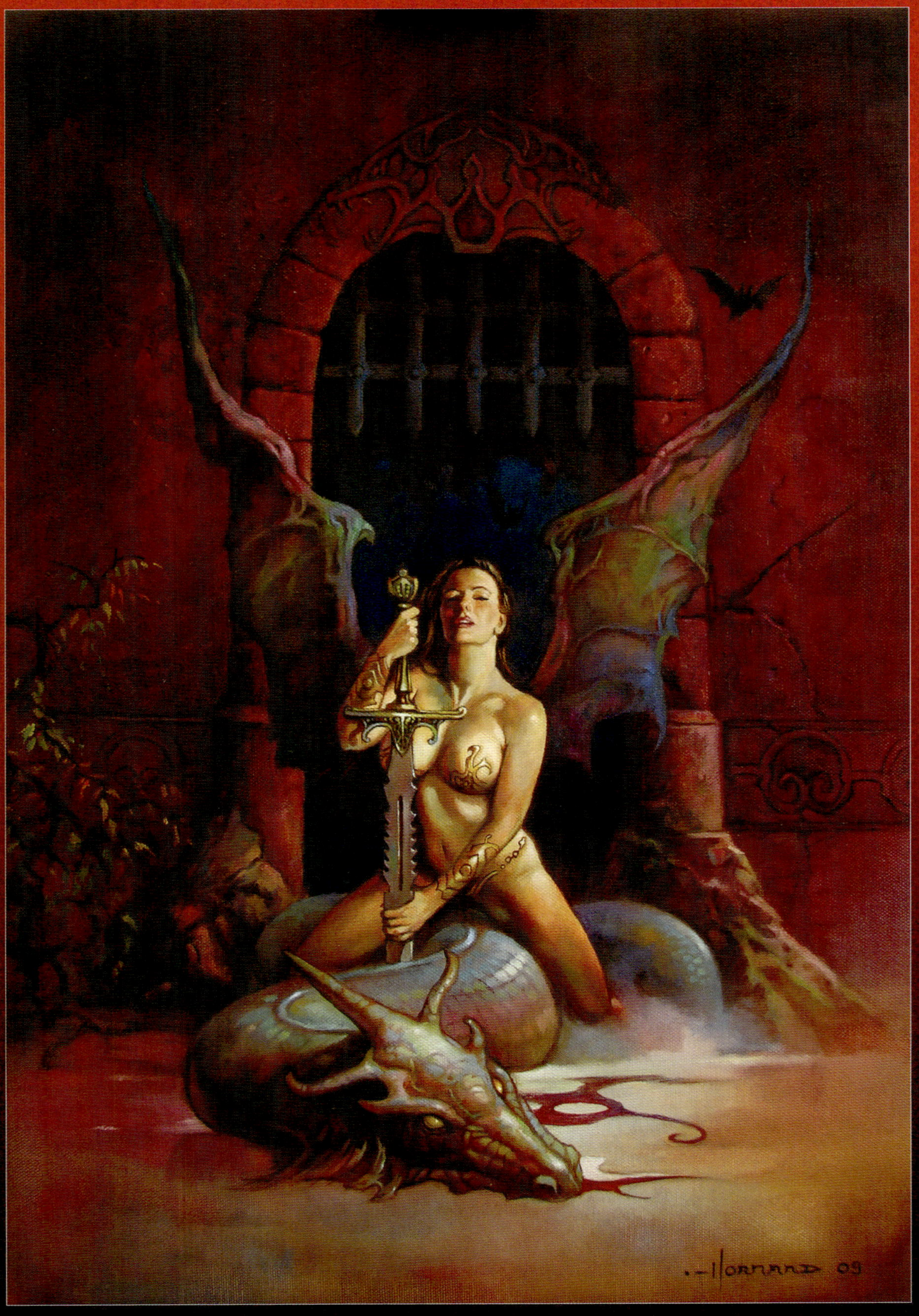

I first selected the image that seemed more aesthetically challenging to me. Then I tried to picture a situation based on both the model's and sword's pose, adding fantasy elements such as the wings and the slayed dragon.

Didier Normand started painting in 1983, he (self) taught himself how to paint by observing the works of Frank Frazetta and Boris Vallejo. A few art shows and a website soon followed and today he is regularly commissioned by publishers

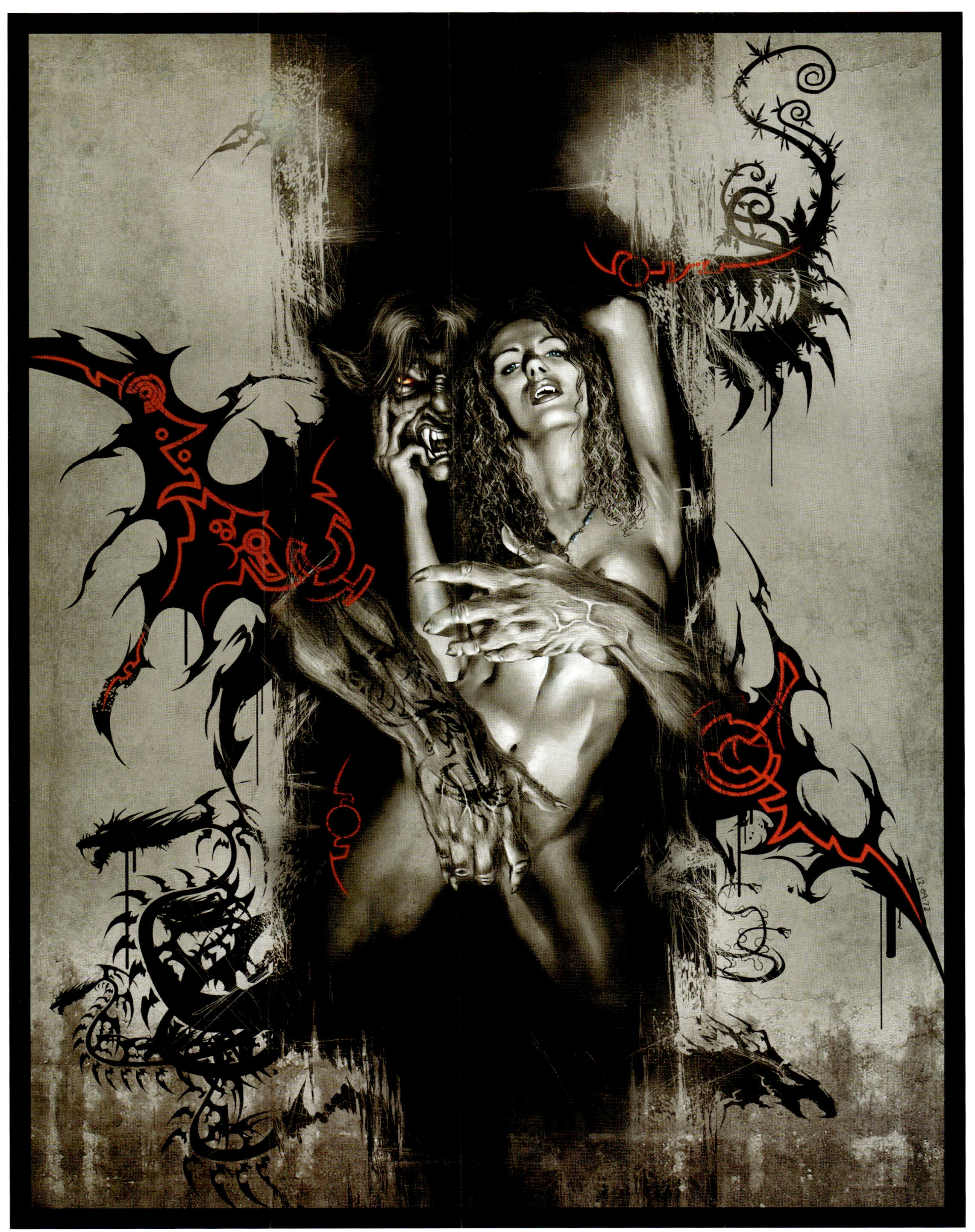

BYRON CASTILLO (Columbia), 2009

Inspired by Shakespeare's novel "Romeo and Juliet" but with an "Underworld" kick.
Byron is a conceptual and textural artist for video games, as well as a 3D and traditional fantasy and sci-fi artist.

SANDRA CHANG ADLAIR (USA), 2009
"Retro Drakaina"

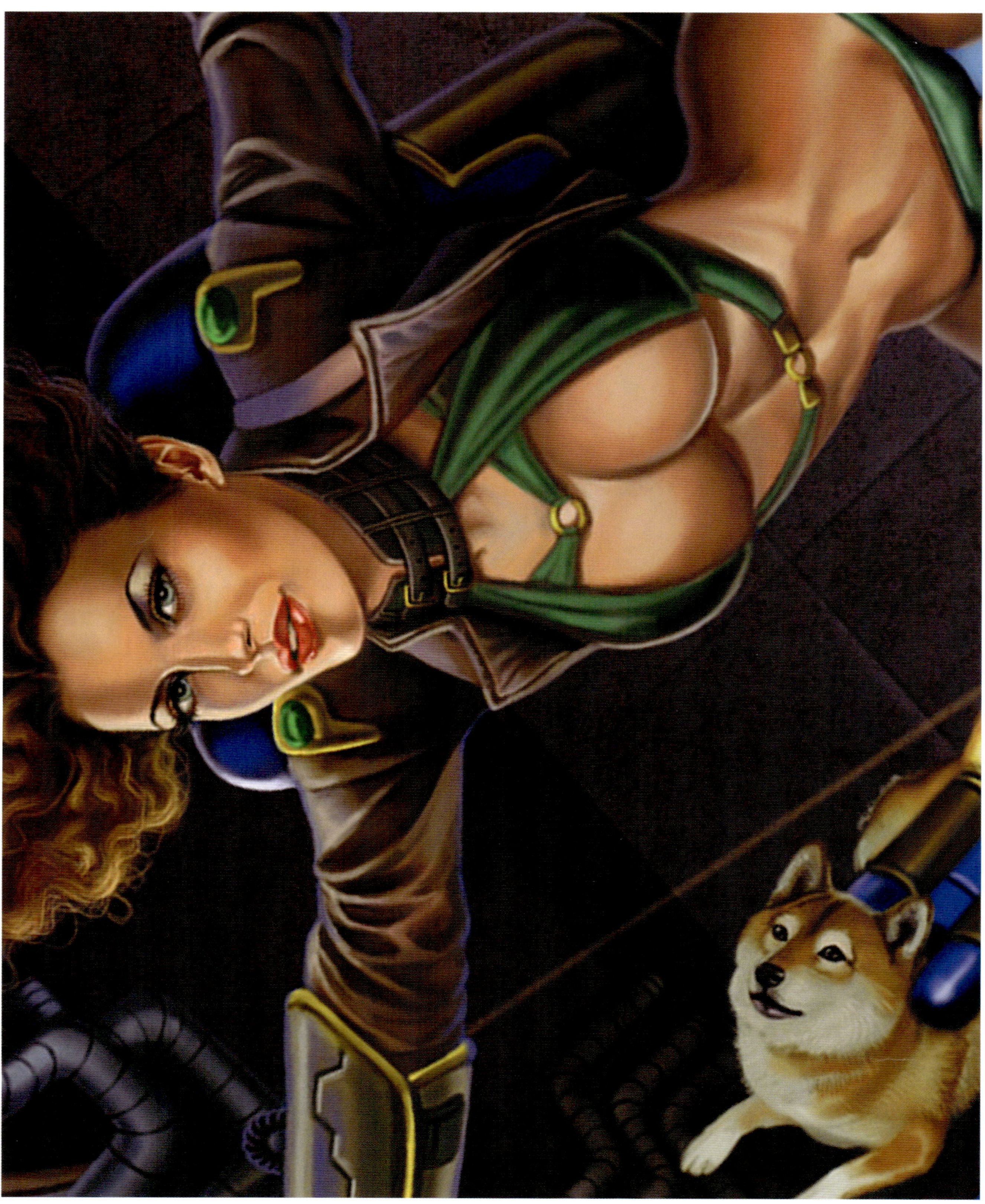

Sandra Chang-Adlair is an illustrator specializing in fantasy and erotic art.
Her preferred method of painting is digital, using Photoshop and Painter.
She made her debut years ago as a comic book artist.
She is currently a pin-up artist for HUSTLER magazine.

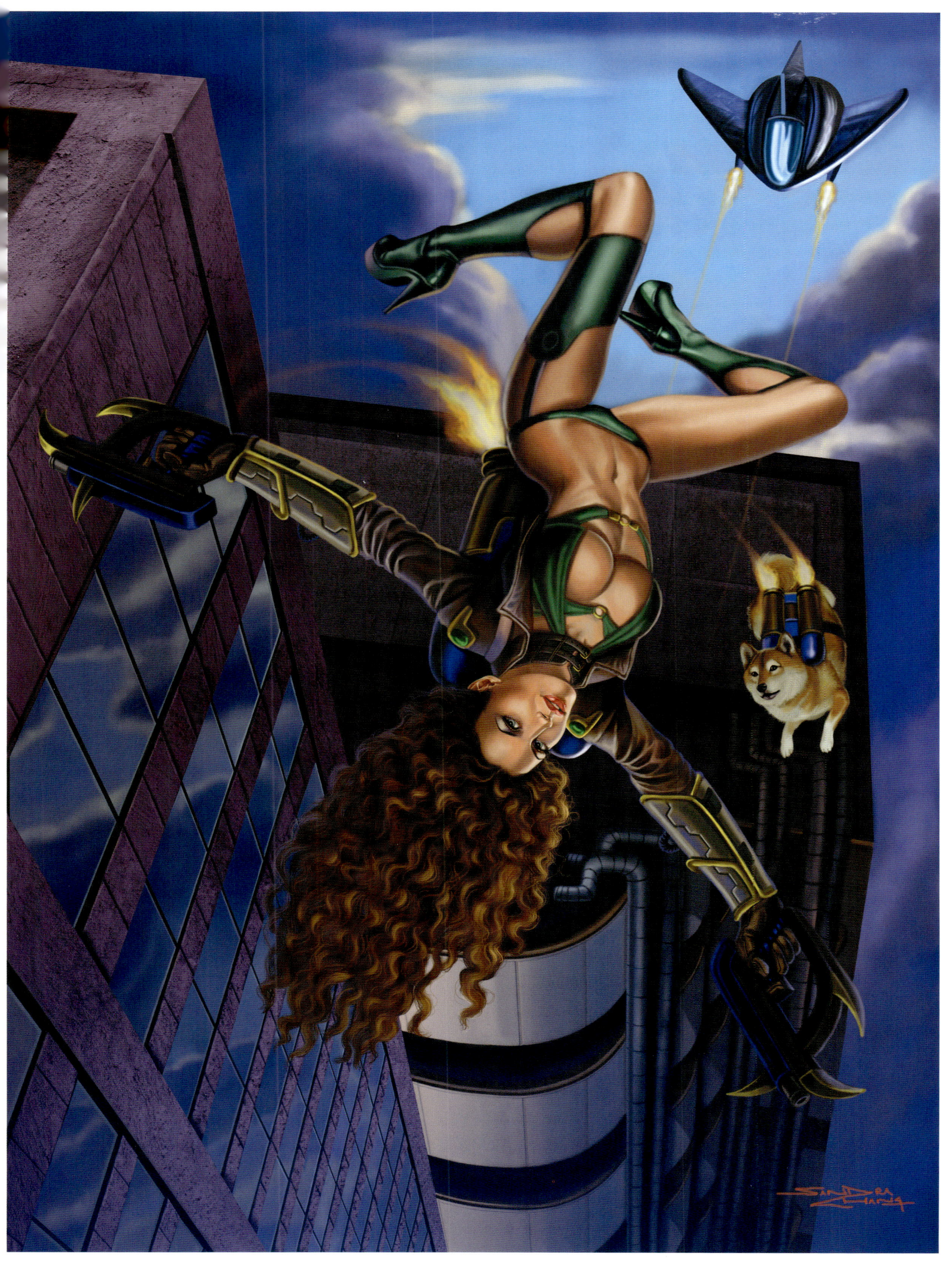

KELLY - X (USA), 2009
"Classic Cheesecake"

Drakaina inspires me with her diversity, beauty and spirit.

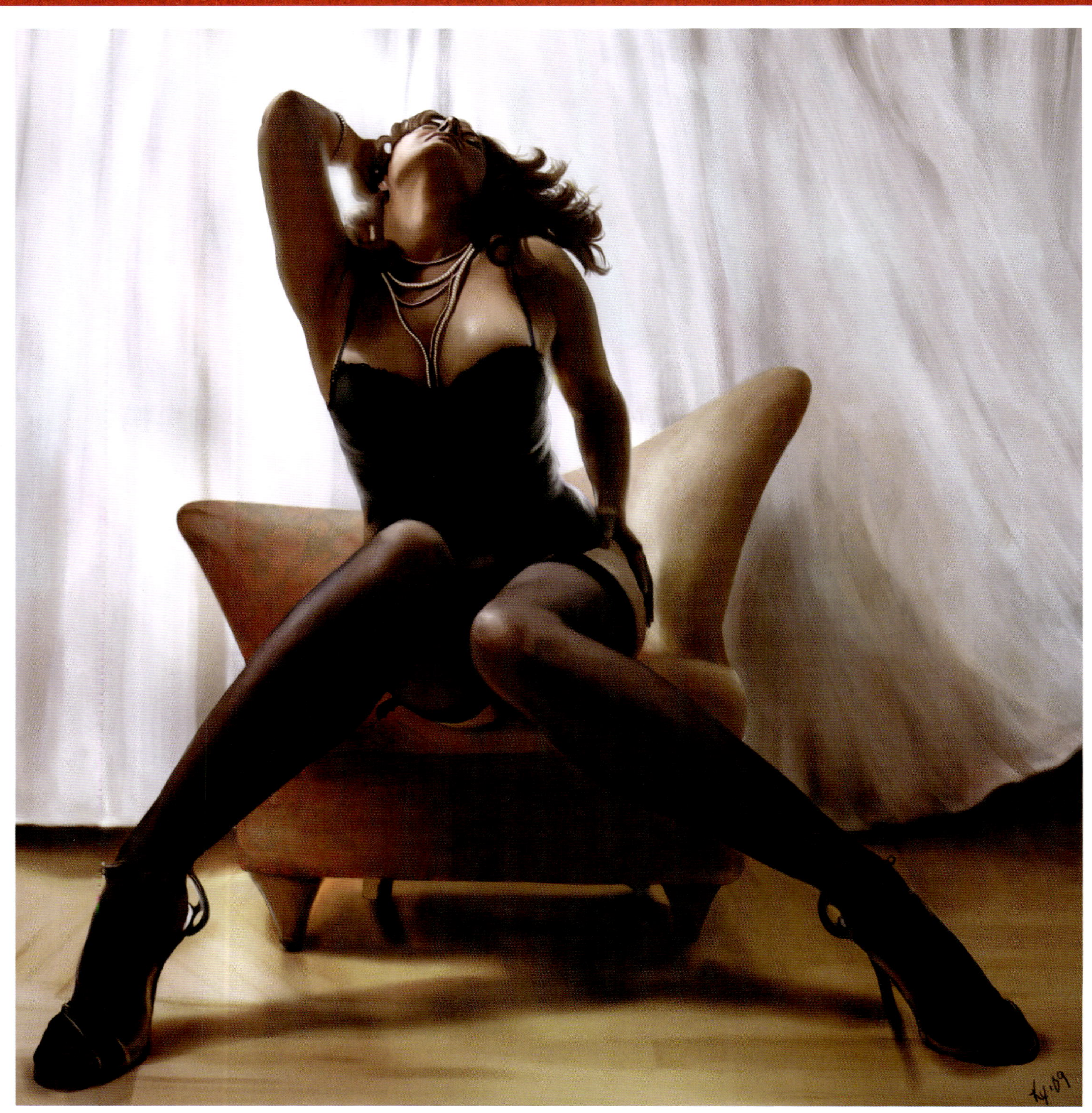

Opposite page
SANDRA CHANG - ADLAIR (USA), 2008

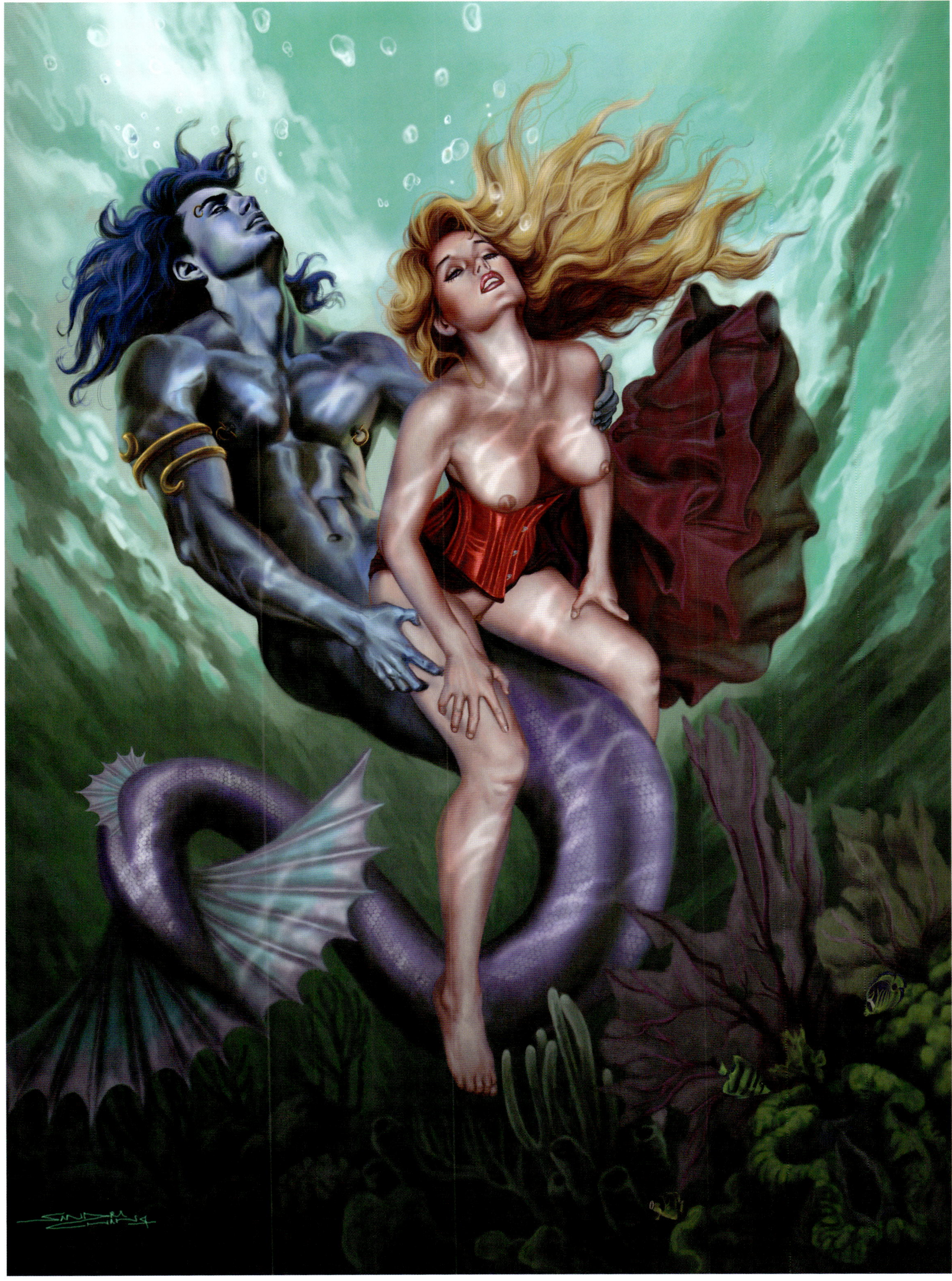

KELLY - X (USA), 2009
"Sailor Girl"

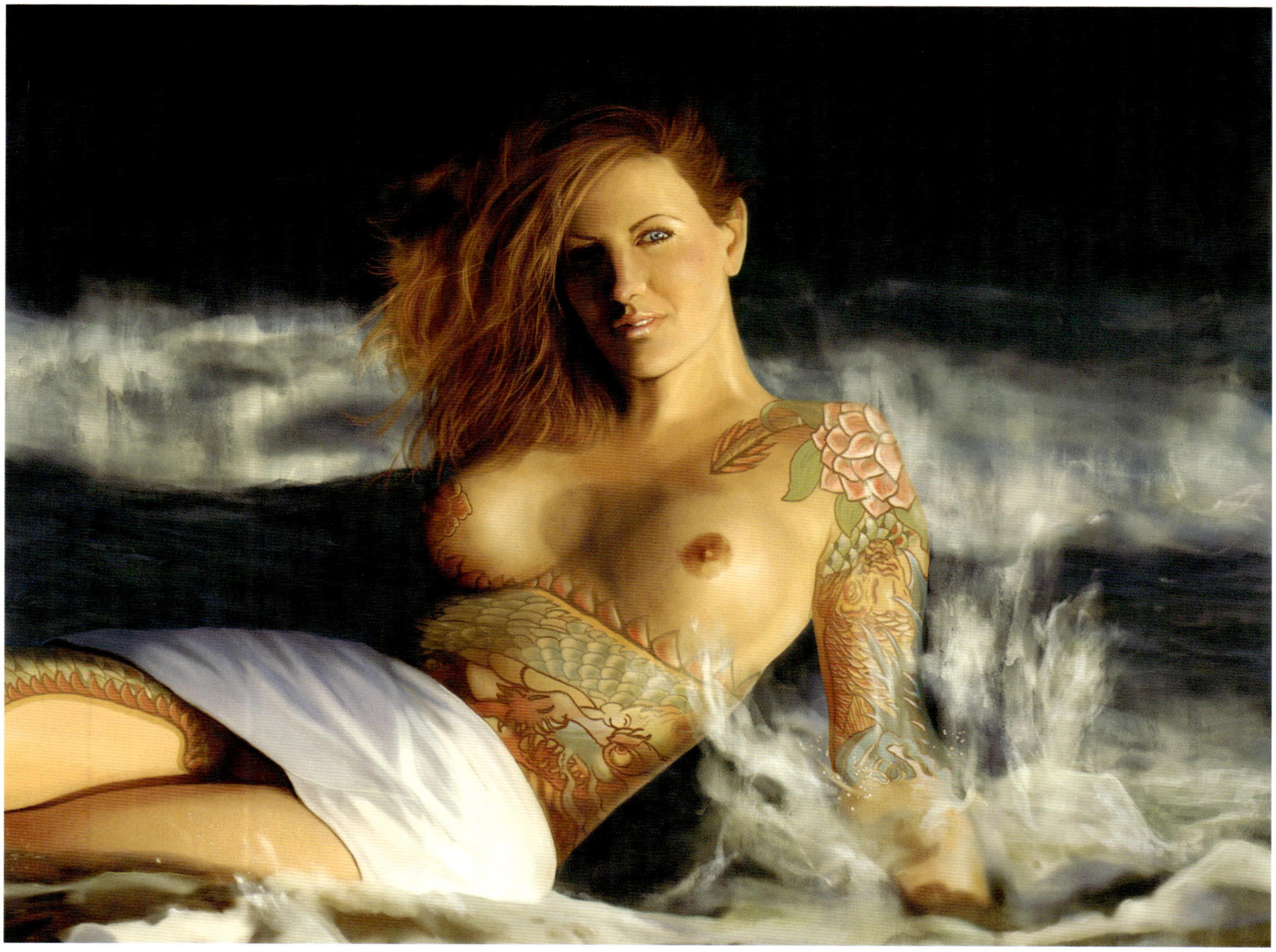

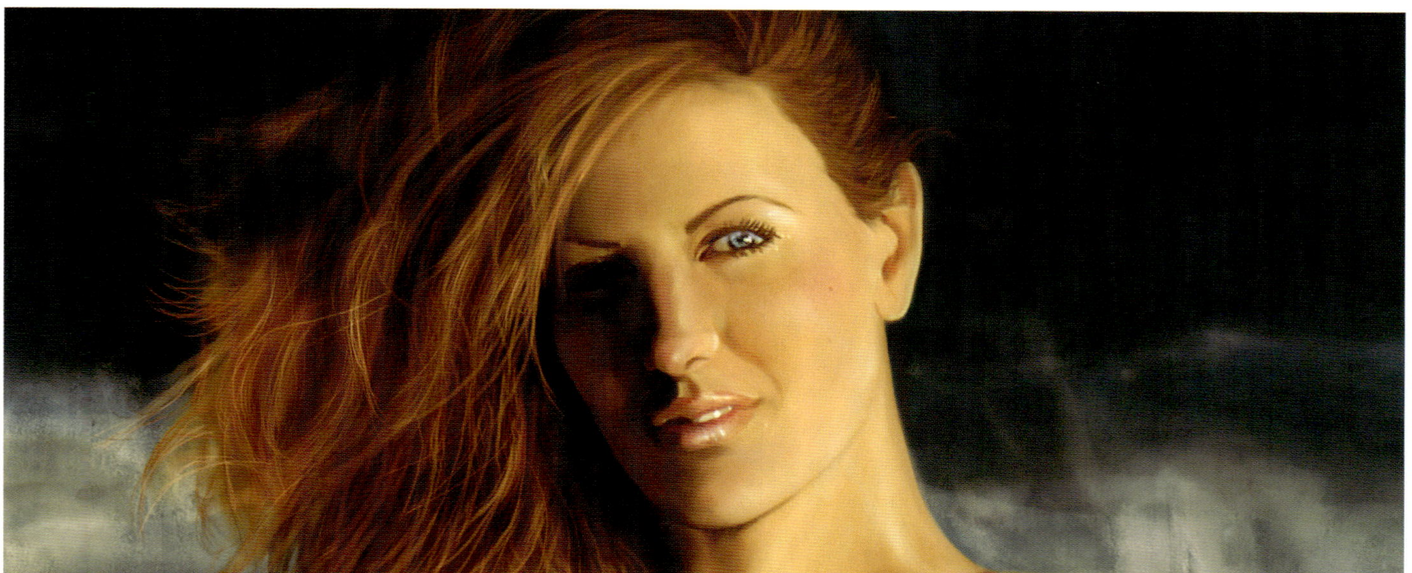

"Sailor Girl" was inspired by the lighting in Drakaina's eyes.

On her art Kelly said "I have tried to establish a modern day pin-up who knows what she wants and feels comfortable enough to be beautiful, self-assured and not afraid to bare it all!"

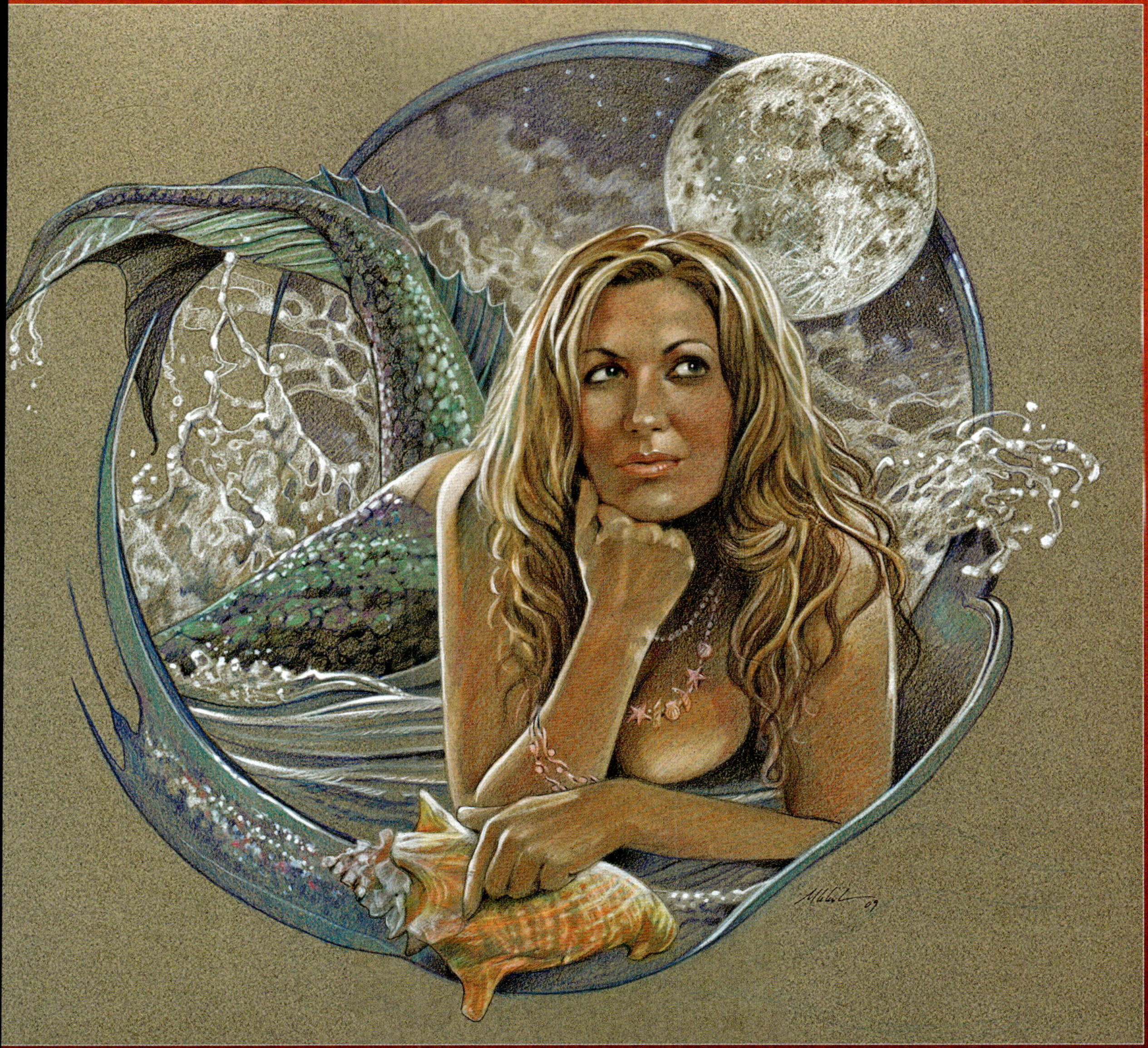

MICHAEL CALANDRA (USA), 2009

Working primarily with airbrush, acrylic paint, and colored pencils, fantasy artist Michael Calandra strives to create images of a dark and haunting nature. Often depicting a commanding and sensuous female figure, he uses dramatic poses, lighting, and color to produce atmospheric settings that reflect the essence of his subjects.

LORENZO DI MAURO (ITALY), 2009

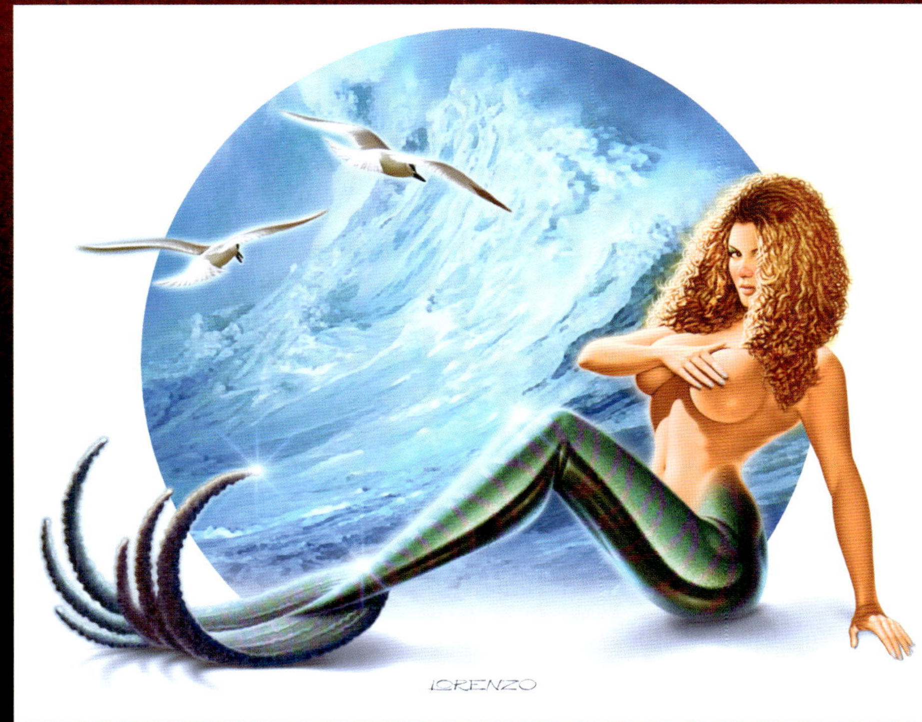

Born in Sicily, Di Mauro began drawing illustrations and comics using both brush and airbrush. Moving to Rome he joined the Illustrators Association, a new group, but a useful starting point to his interest in creating pin-up work, one of his final images actually having Elvgren's name as part of the background.
The 80's saw his work widely recognized through the advertising market, with his almost photorealistic technique.
The 90's had him experimenting with the digital imaging process, something that in 2001 became his primary choice for creating artwork.
He continued using the original tools of brush and airbrush, creating vivid images with his use of acrylic paints. Now that his proficiency has improved with the graphics tablet, unless it's a private commissioned piece, the less inclined he is to work with traditional methods .

RENEE BIERTEMPFEL (USA), 2009
"Muse of Creation"

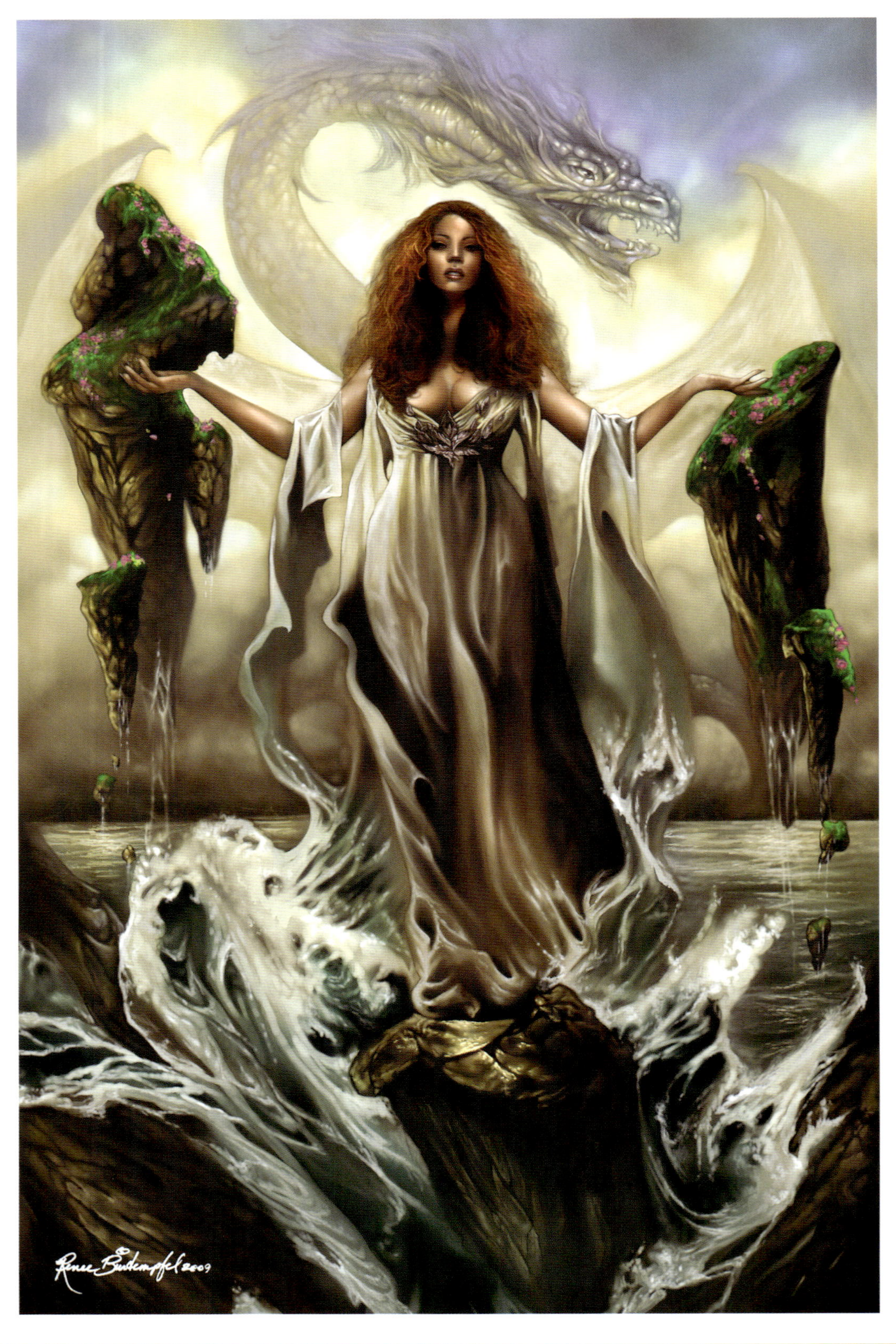

What inspired this piece for me is that Drakaina is a source of inspiration to artists out there hence I see her as a "Muse of Creation" symbolized in the painting as a creation goddess. The dragon above in the clouds represents the meaning of her name.

Renee Biertempfel has been a graphic artist and illustrator for 18 years having worked in various parts of the art industry. She is now illustrating children's books and painting and selling her own works which have been licensed as products sold around the world.

DAVID MICHAEL WRIGHT (England), 2009
"Drakaina, in the Lands of Fantasy"

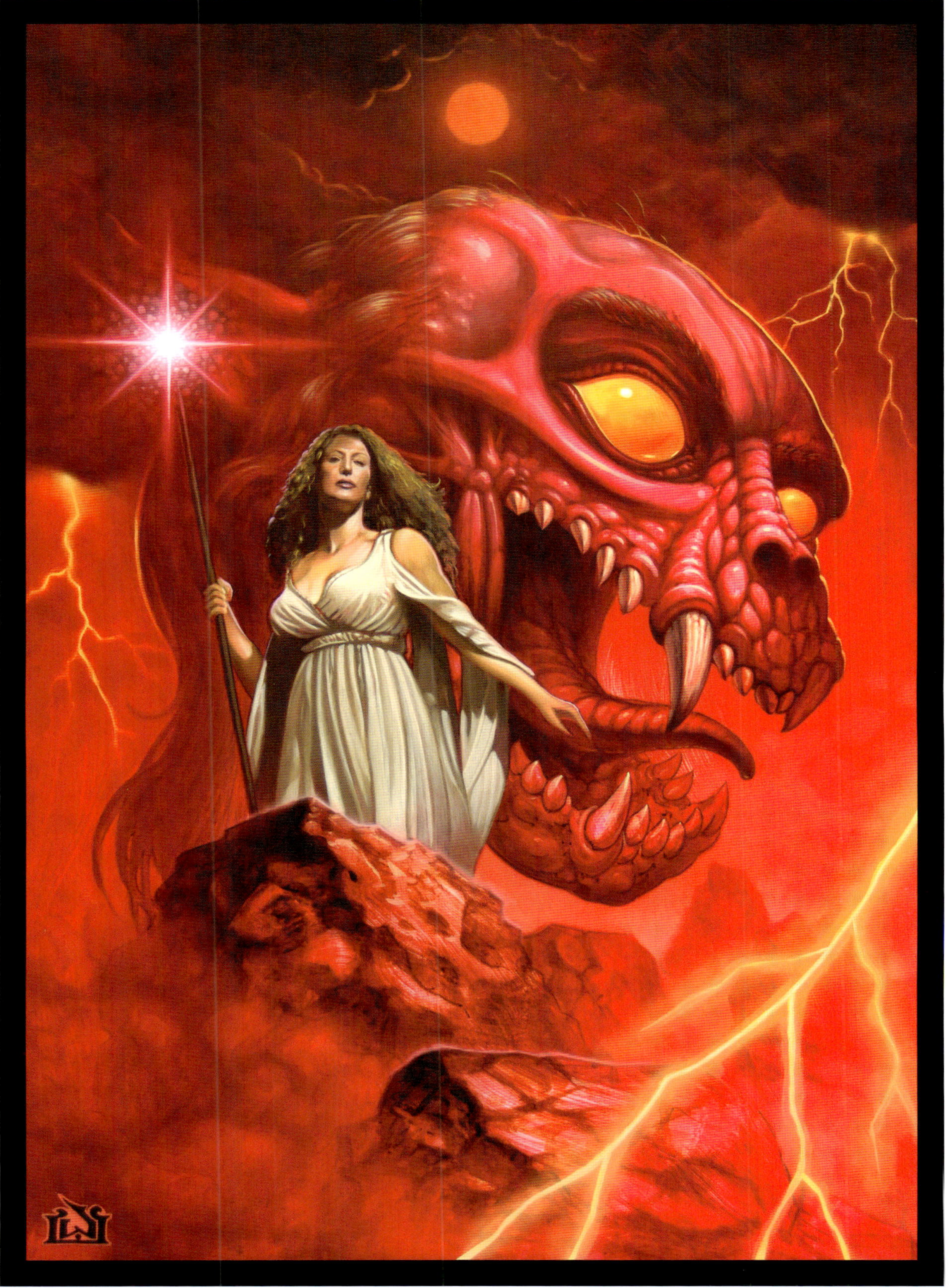

"When browsing the Drakaina photo archives for inspiration, I came across the main reference image I was to use for this artwork. I really liked the air of defiance and mastery about it, and the idea for the painting followed almost instantly."

David Michael Wright was born in 1979, and lives in South Yorkshire, England. He works as a freelance illustrator specializing in fantasy, sci-fi & RPG art.

DARKER REALMS

SCARLET GOTHICA (Italy), 2009
"Golden Bathory"
In this picture, I wanted to represent the beautiful Drakaina as the weird countess Erzsébet Bathory, during one of her notorious blood baths. Generally this character is represented with a dark and bleak background, in macabre and vampiric attitudes; but this time I wanted to play with warm colors and "baroque" sensations, as to express pleasure, lust and opulence that the countess felt when she had her sacrilegious bath.

Claudia was born in 1982 in Rieti, a small Italian medieval town, under the Appennino range, enclosed by the nearer beautiful forests and by an evergreen landscape. She attended the Classics School in Rieti, being keen on ancient literatures, Greek and Roman mythology, and in particular Italian art history, as she was drawing even more. She then graduated in Architecture at the Roma TRE University, and has been attending the Scuola Internazionale di Comics in Rome, a professional school for illustrators since 2006.

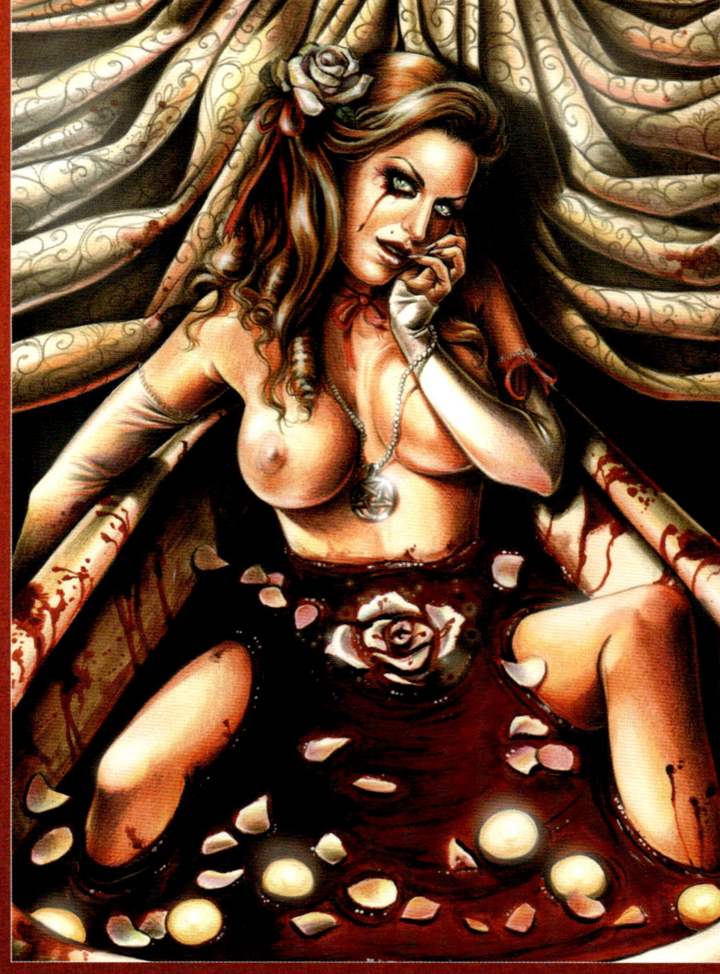

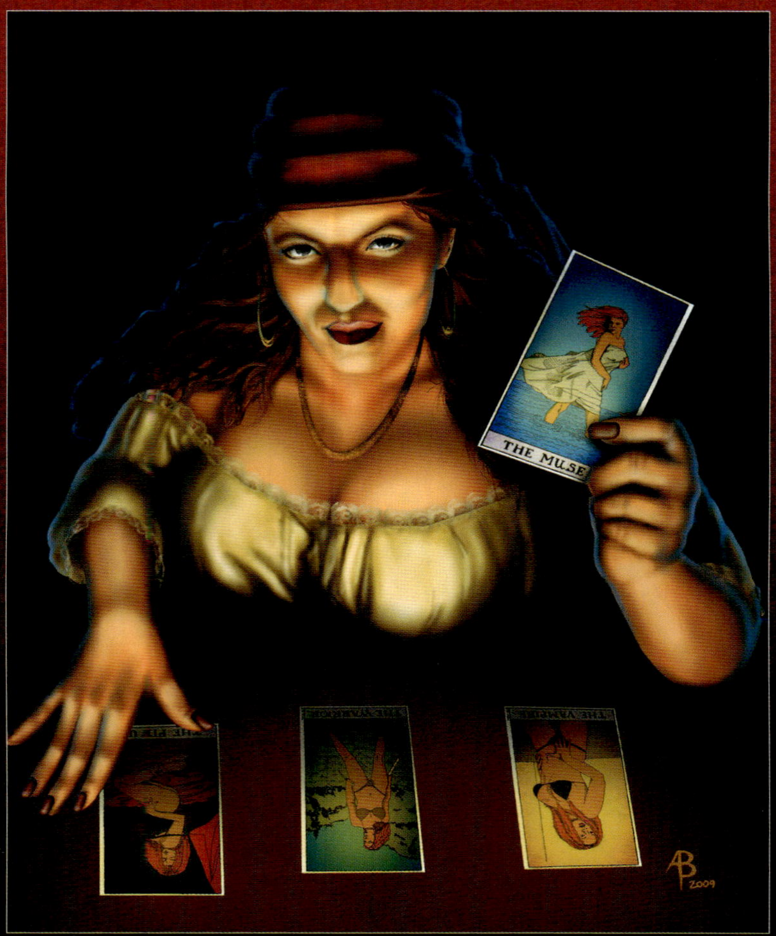

ADAM BRAUM (USA), 2009
"Role Playing"
My inspiration was that I wanted to do a piece that really played on Drakaina's role as an artist's muse and how she interchanges between characters depending on the artist's subject.

Adam Braun is an artist that made the transition from inking comic books to drawing and painting pin-ups, creating sexy images both traditionally and digitally. His art focuses on capturing the sensuality and emotion of his subjects through realistic use of light and shadow.

Opposite page:
BAM-BAM (USA), 2009
"Drakaina Succubus"
A succubus is a demon who takes the form of a highly attractive woman to seduce men . From looking at Drakaina's gallery it was clear she had that seducing quality combined with a cheeky wickedness.

To improve my figurative work I recently set about painting pin-ups. I researched pin-up artists past and present and in doing so really gained an admiration for the skill of the artists in capturing the female form and all its character from fun to sexy and everything in between.

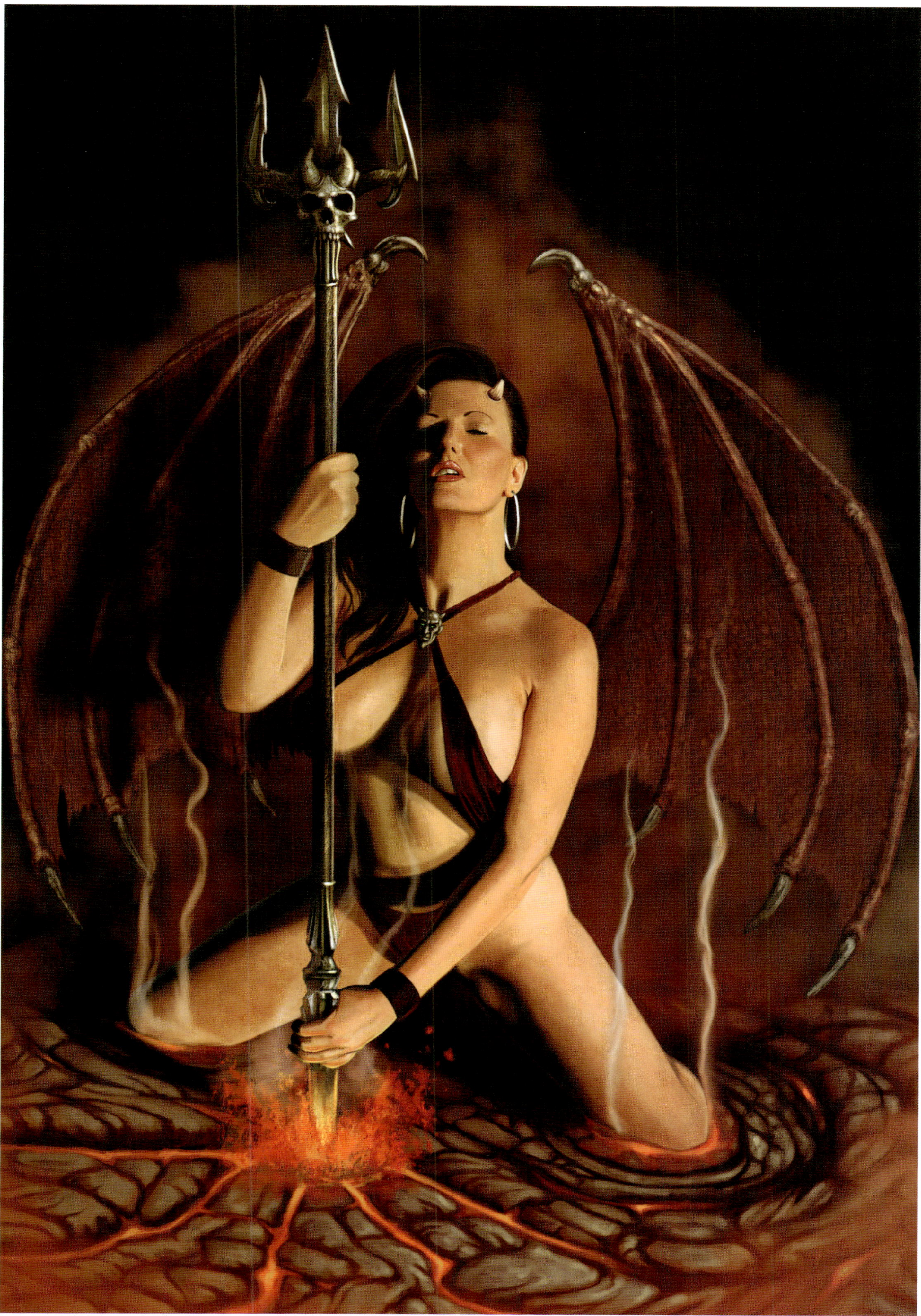

TCHAL & DOLE (France), 2009

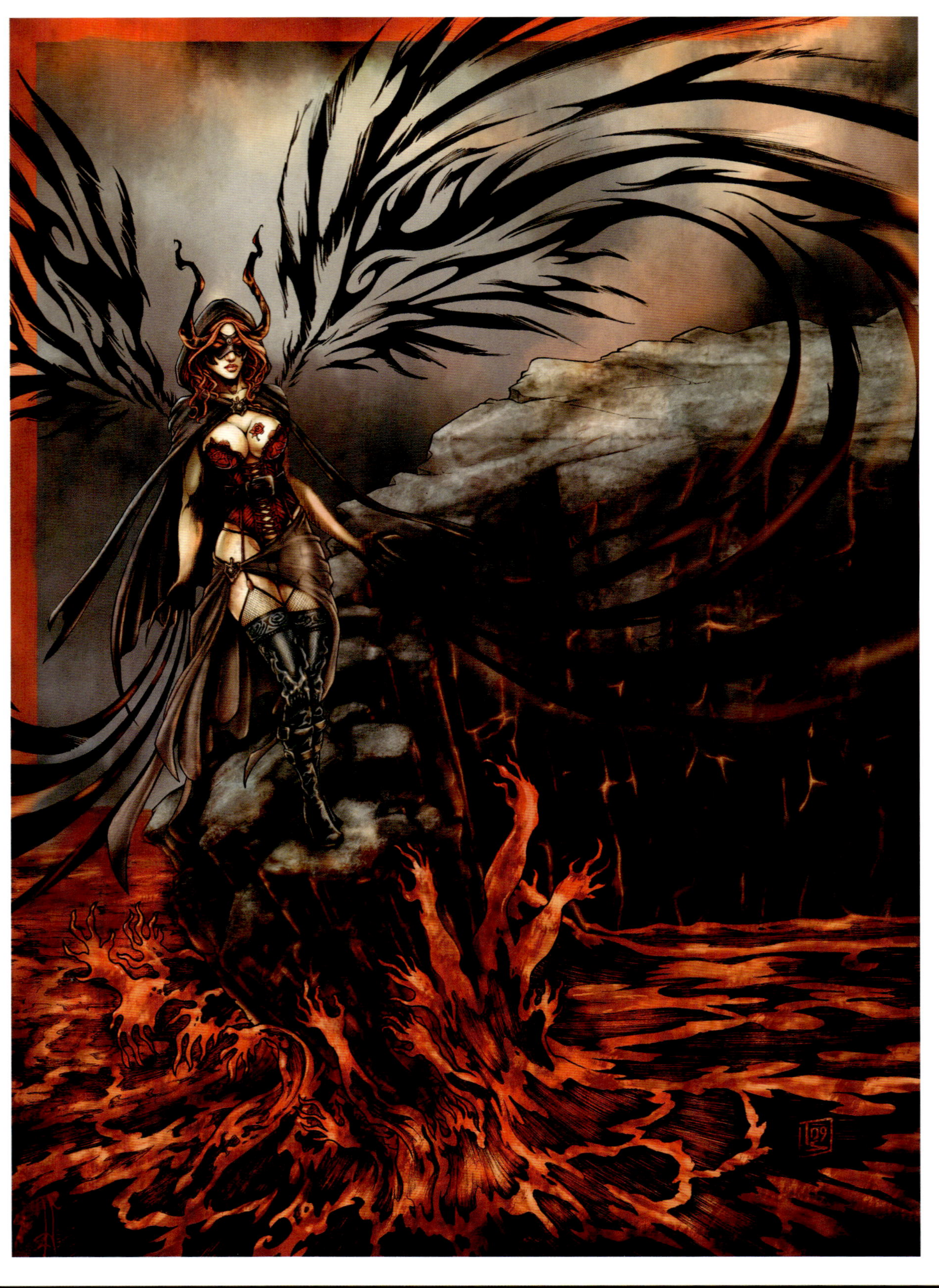

This page:

"Ailes Obscures"

I wanted to draw a darker piece for Drakaina in which she would be dark herself. But even a child from darkness wants to rise toward the light, despite the hands trying to hold her back and take her in deeper

Opposite page:

"On the Way"

Tchal lives in the Parisian suburbs where he uses his free time to draw and perfect his techniques

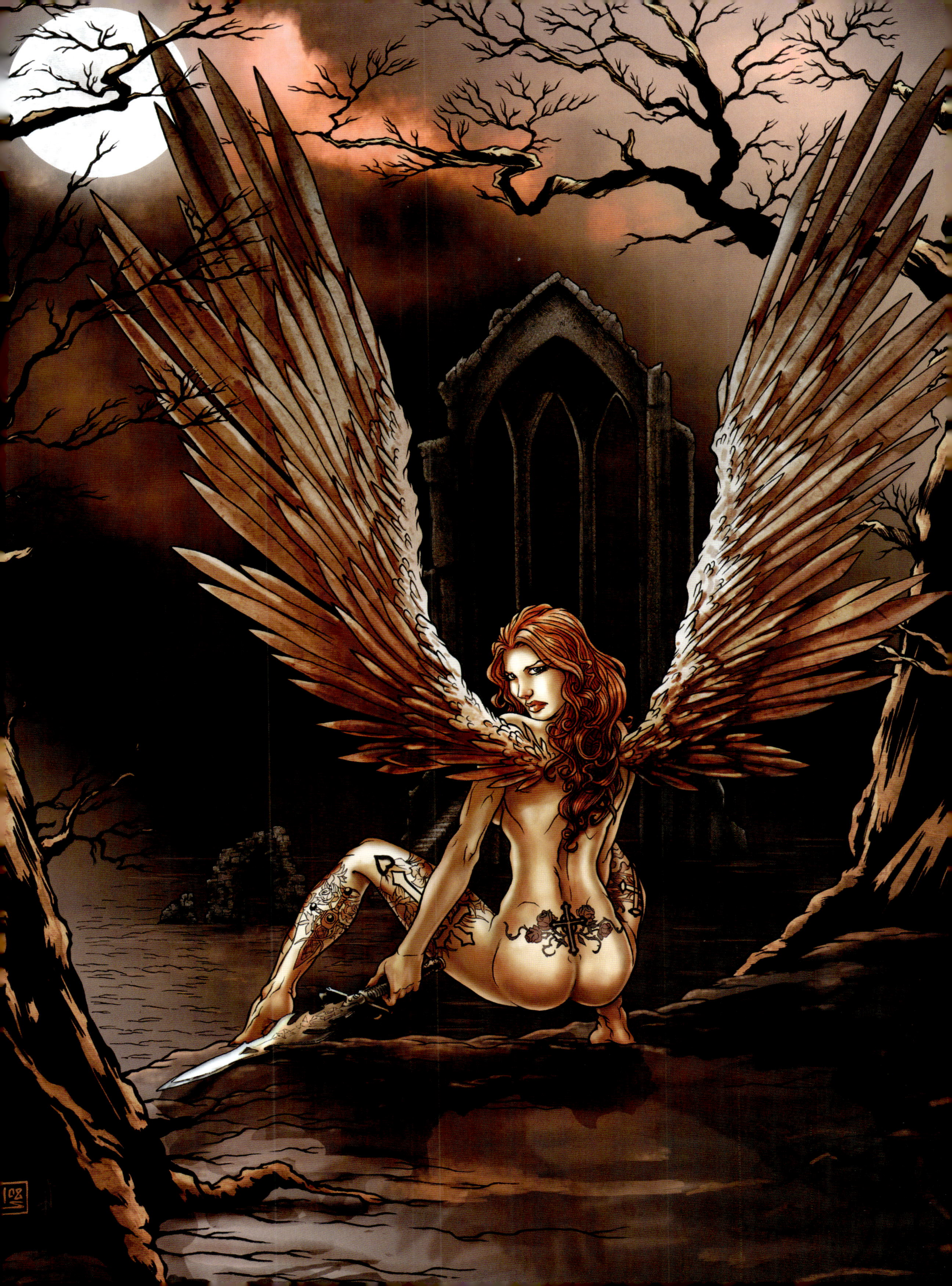

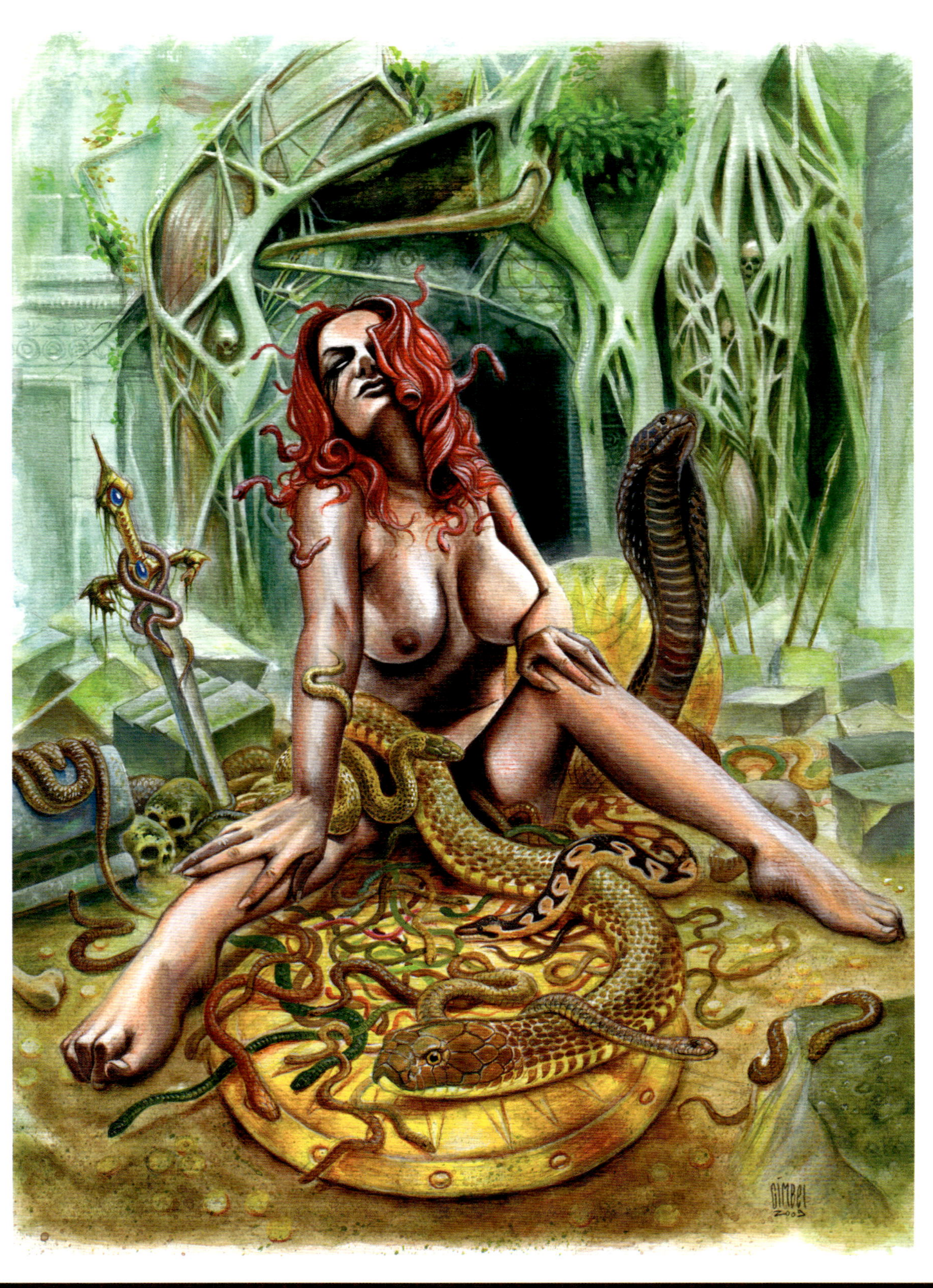

ALEXANDRE GRIMBEL, (France), 2009
"Medusa"

I saw in Drakaina's sultry attitude an invitation, a spell that a simple mortal couldn't free himself from. In her massive mane are rings of snakes mingling with her curls. A femme fatale, as dangerous as she is attractive.

Born on April 8th, 1982 in Alsace France, Alexandre has been drawing since his early years. His imagination fed with comic books and fantastic art books, he fell in love with the world of fantasy art. Graphic designer by trade, he now leaps into the world of freelancing.

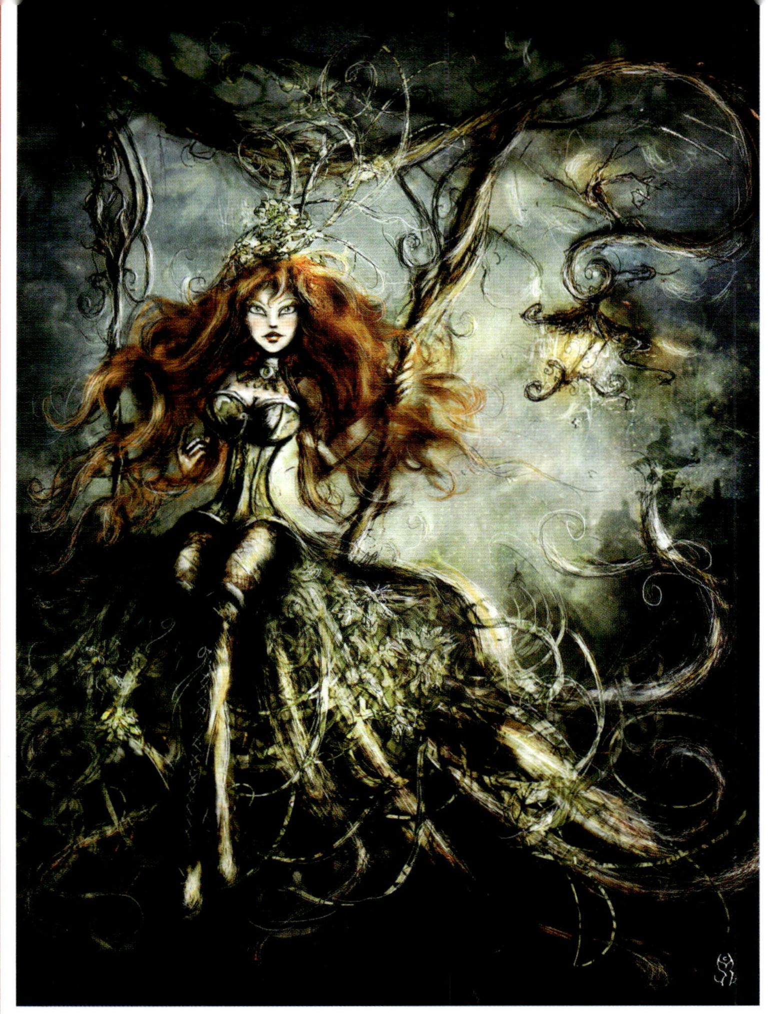

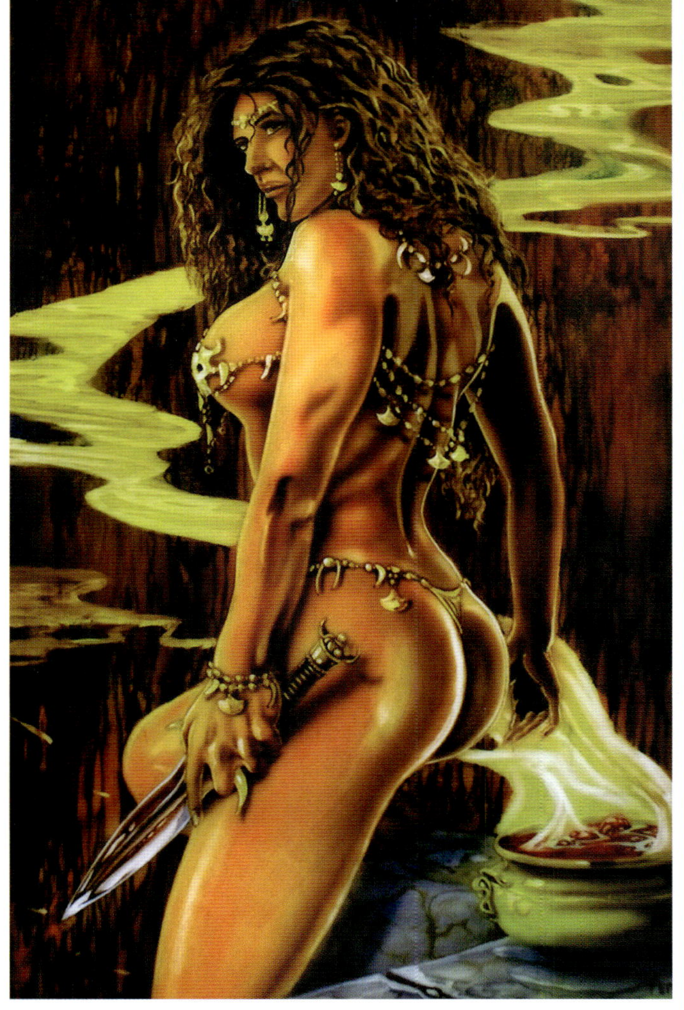

SANDRINE REPLAT (FRANCE), 2009"
"Drakaina Fairy Queen"
Artwork inspired by the Drakaina's Samhain gallery, the one with the flowing white gown. You can feel such harmony with nature, that I went for this side of Drakaina's personality, as it is also close to my own.

Born in Grenoble, in the Alps, nature is her inspiration. She is a dark traditional and digital artist. Her art is a study in light and shadow. Sandrine uses and mixes different mediums to make her paintings : pencil, ink, charcoal pen, acrylic or watercolor, and often finishes the details, the work of light and contrast in Photoshop. She likes to explore all the possibilities of the different mediums used. She suggests more than she shows by playing with the light and huge contrast, to convey a vision of the world close to childhood's nightmares yet filled with fairies.

JOHNNEY W. PERKINS (USA), 2009
"Drakaina"
Discovering Frank Frazetta at the age 5, Johnney has been a fan of fantasy ever since, whether it was the art, or the literature of such authors as Edgar Rice Burroughs and Robert E. Howard. Johnney has been an attending guest at many fantasy, sci-fi and comic book conventions for the past 12 years, along with producing commercial artwork and commissions in every medium. He has now found a home with Rogue Blades Entertainment as Artist Acquisitioner and doing what he loves – producing artwork for a group that has brought "pulp" back the way he remembers it.

PIERLUIGI ABBONDANZA (Italy), 2009
"Little Red Riding Drak"
Freelance illustrator, character designer and colorist who has worked for clients like Bianca Beauchamp, Marketa Belonoha, RPG Games, GG Studio (comics), as well as many private commissions. He likes to create characters and environments, and horror and fantasy scenarios are his favorite subjects.

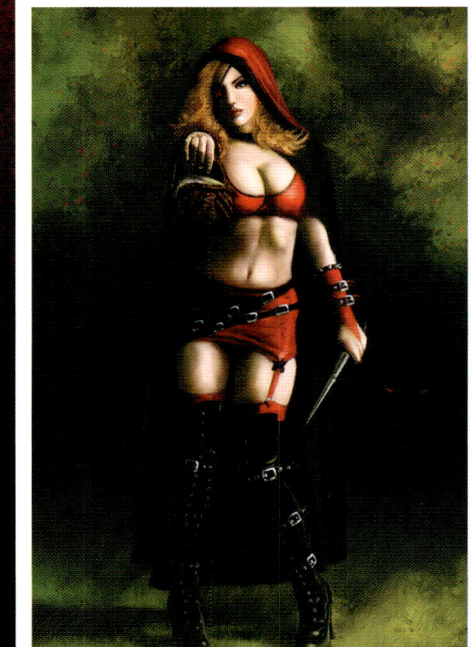

DRAKAINA MANGA STLYE

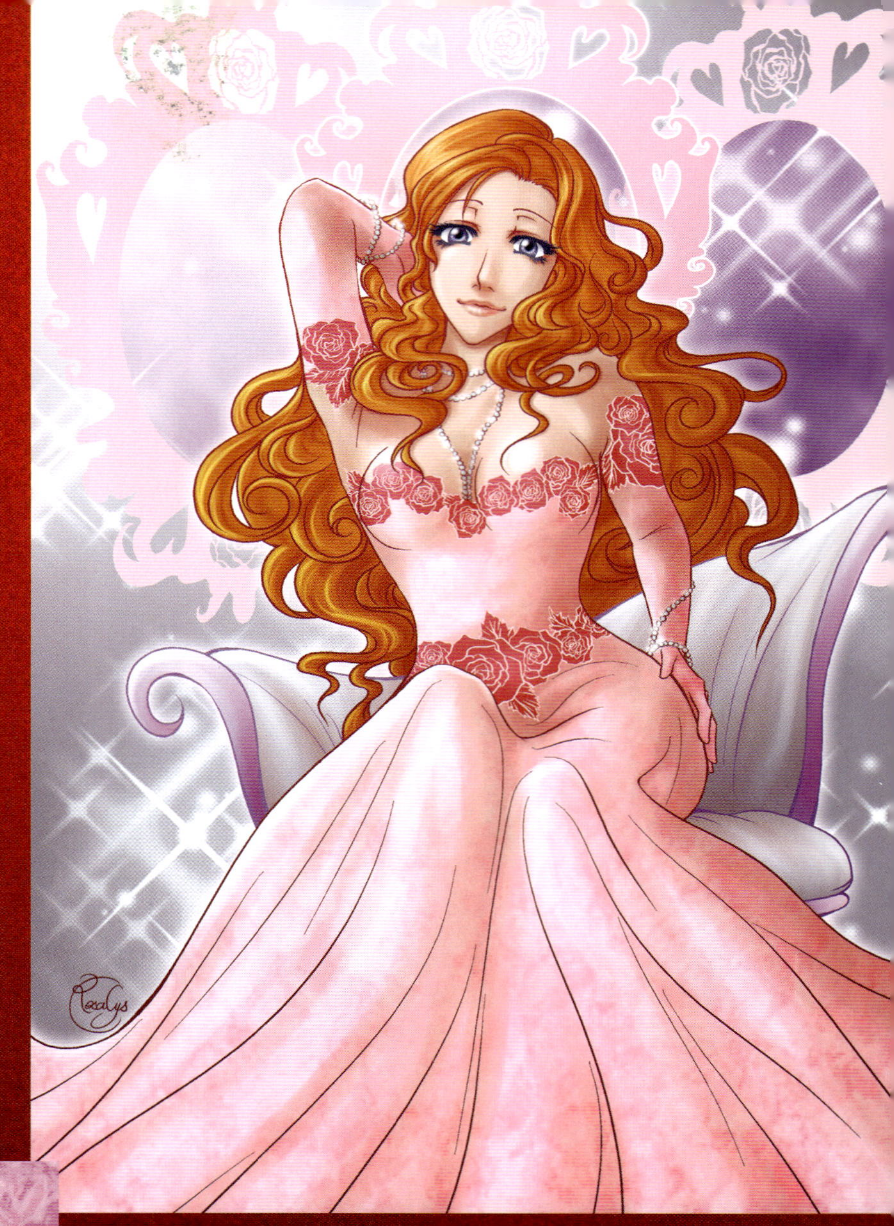

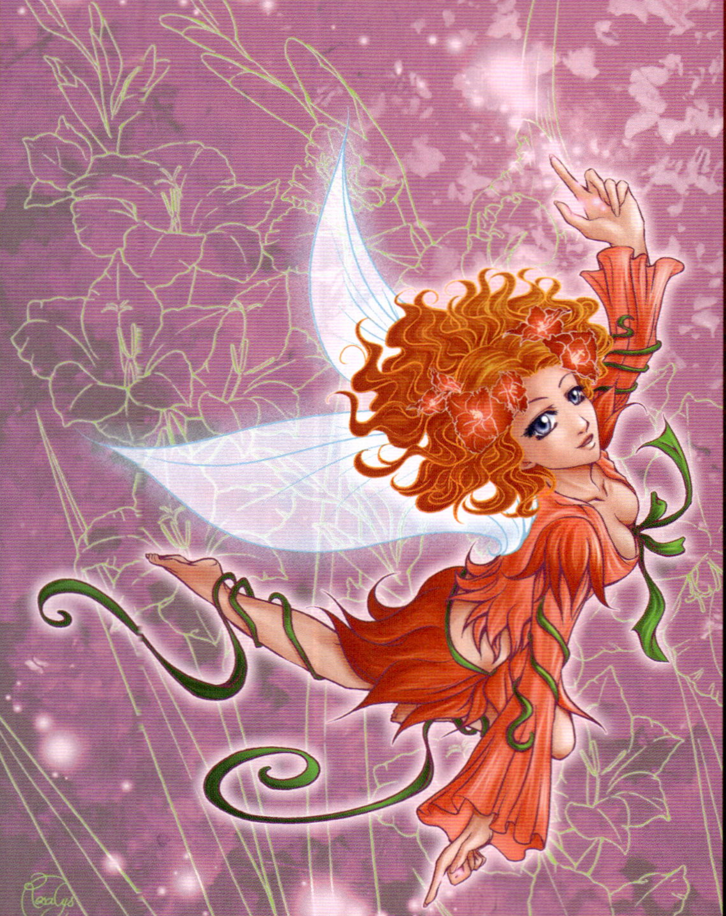

ROSALYS (France), 2009

French from birth but Japanese at heart, Rosalys is a comic book artist and author. She mainly draws beautiful and feminine women in a cheerful and positive atmosphere, to express the sensibility of long hair caressing the neck, or the delicacy of a kiss on a flower petal.

Top:
"Princesse de la Beauté"
The first thought that came to my mind when I saw Drakaina's pictures was "Oh my.. she is gorgeous". I then naturally wanted t represent her as a Princess surrounded by roses, her beauty shining through and her hair falling in a cascade of curls.

Left:
"L'envol d'une fée"
More to represent Drakaina's beauty.
What makes flowers so pretty ?
A beautiful fairy's magic!

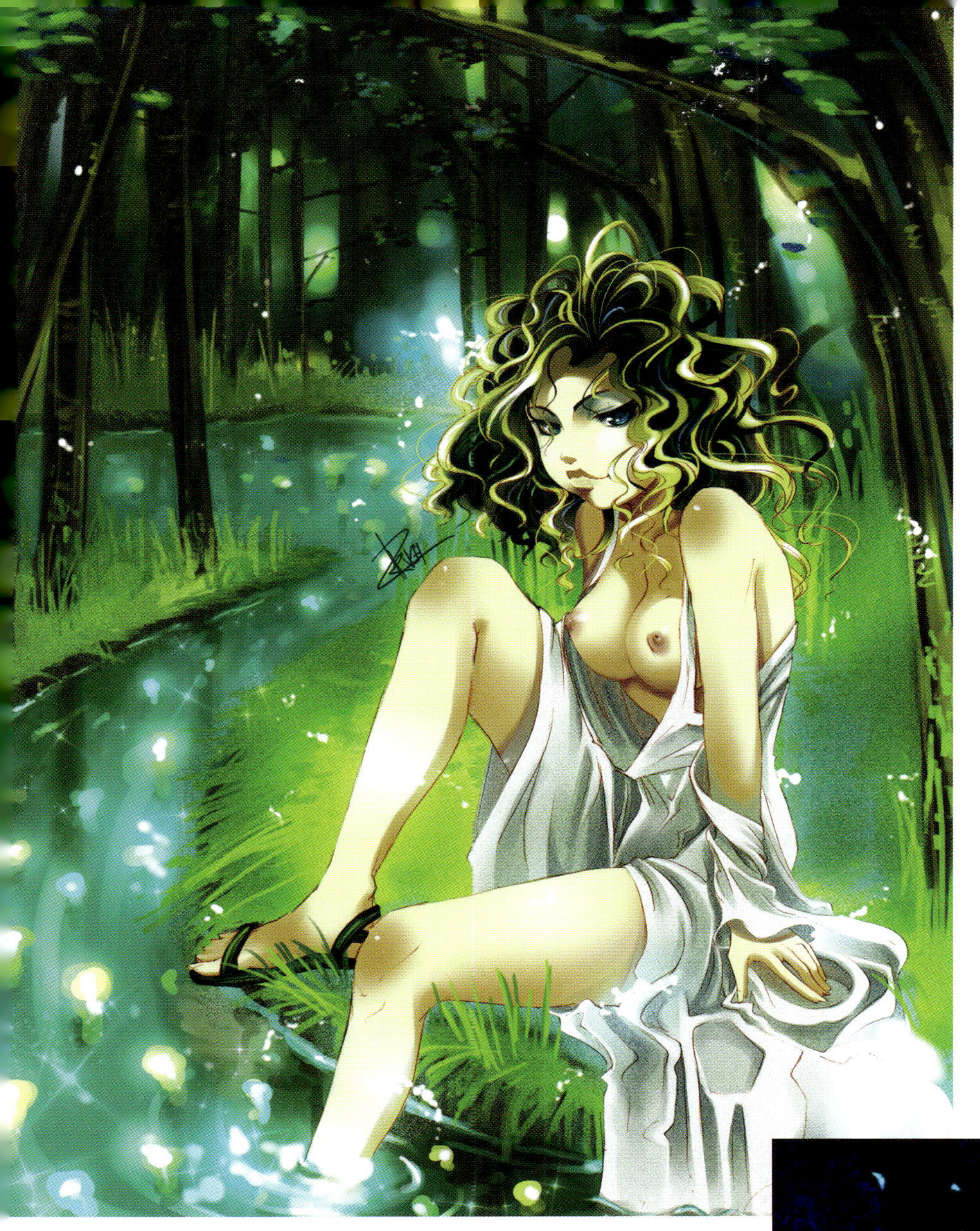

PRUSH (Thailand), 2009
"Queen of the Fireflies"

In this artwork I wanted Drakaina to look like a nymph or a forest fairy, especially because of her hair. I also found the white witch fantasy gown was perfectly suited for Drakaina.

Prush is a 20 years old artist from Bangkok specialized in anime style drawings.

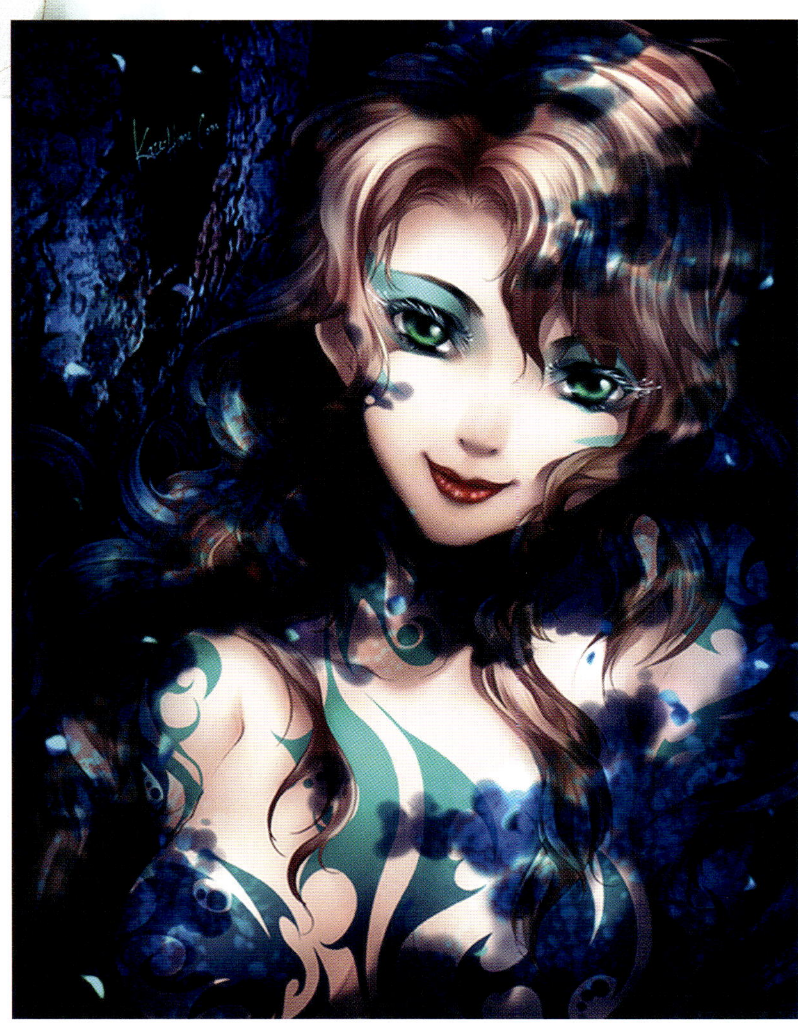

KAZE-HINE (Canada), 2009
"Drakaina"

Rather than the intense hot colors I saw in the references, I wanted to draw Drakaina in an elegant, mystical, and cool demeanor.

Born May 2nd, 1990, a self-taught artist and founder of Kaze-Hime Co. She specializes in computer graphic illustration, and has a vast knowledge of Photoshop.

FABRIZIO PASINI
(Italy), 2009
"Drakaina"

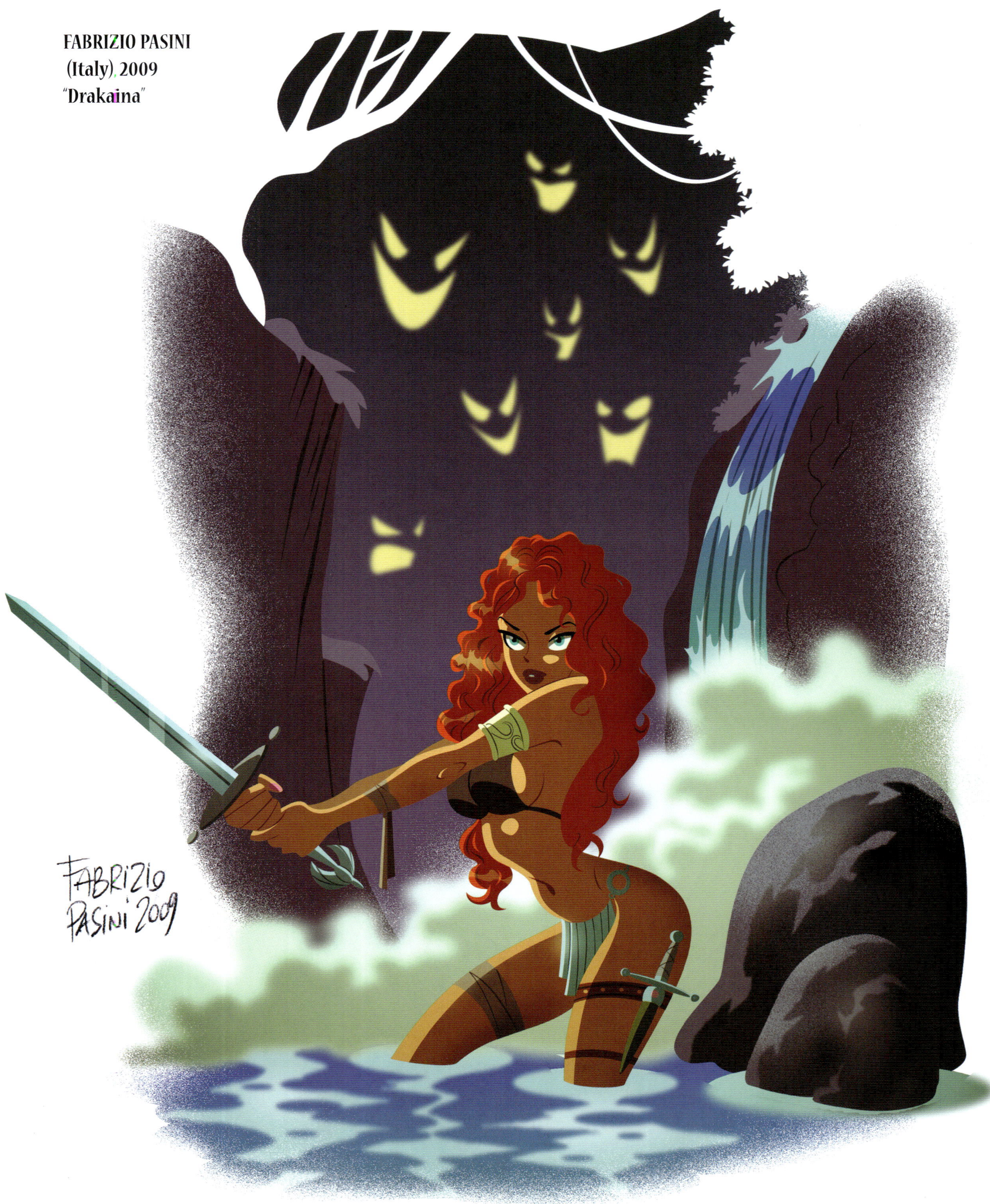

Italian comic artist, triple-threat penciller, inker and colorist, Fabrizio has been published in several comics and art books worldwide. His distinctive sexy cartoon style made him a favorite amongst glamour models.

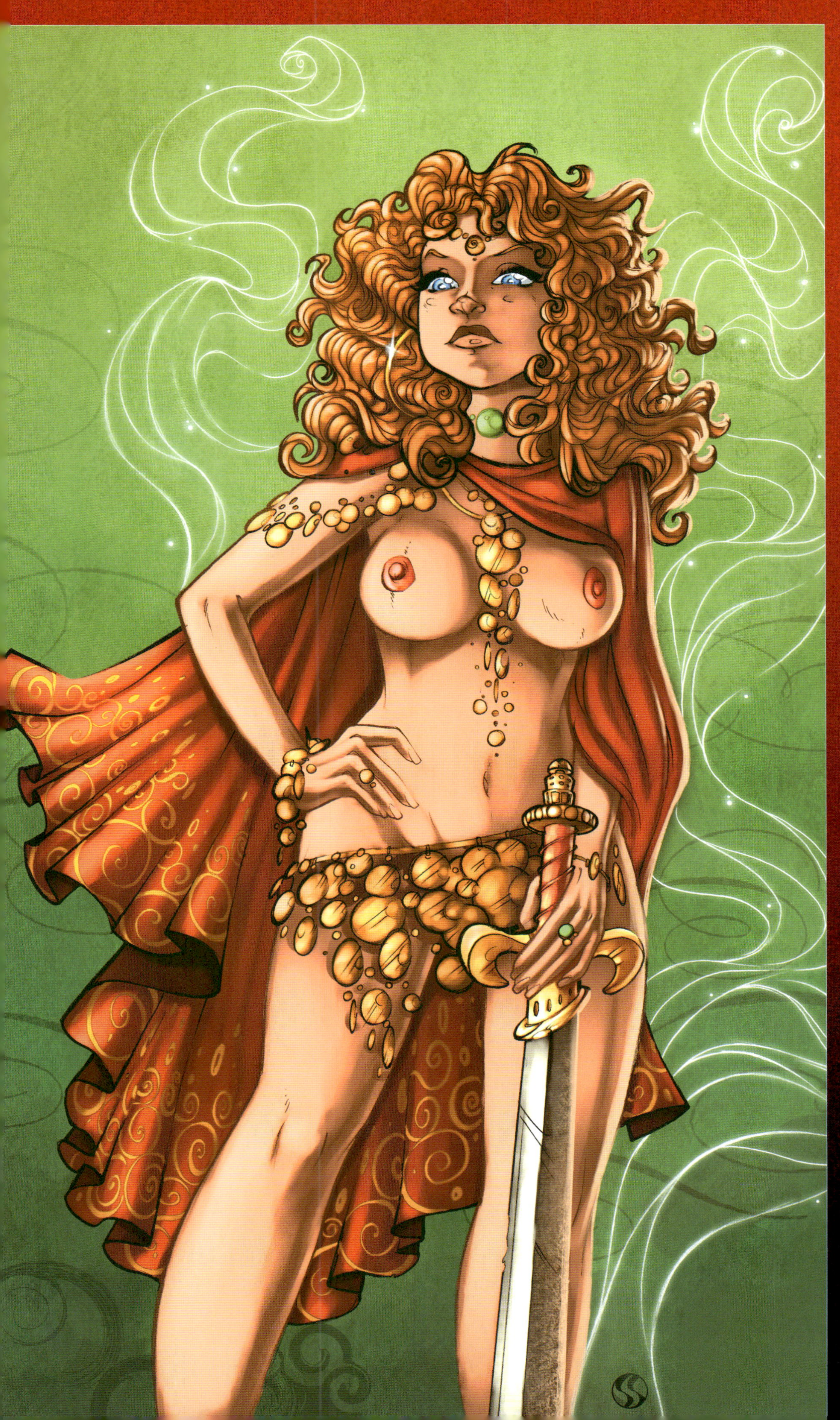

OOD SERRIERE
(France), 2009

"Drakaina Warrior"

Both a comic book author and artist, Ood Serriere is a young woman whose work can been seen in a number of French comic books (SWEET SOCELLERY, in which she participated with other creators being the latest) and art books.

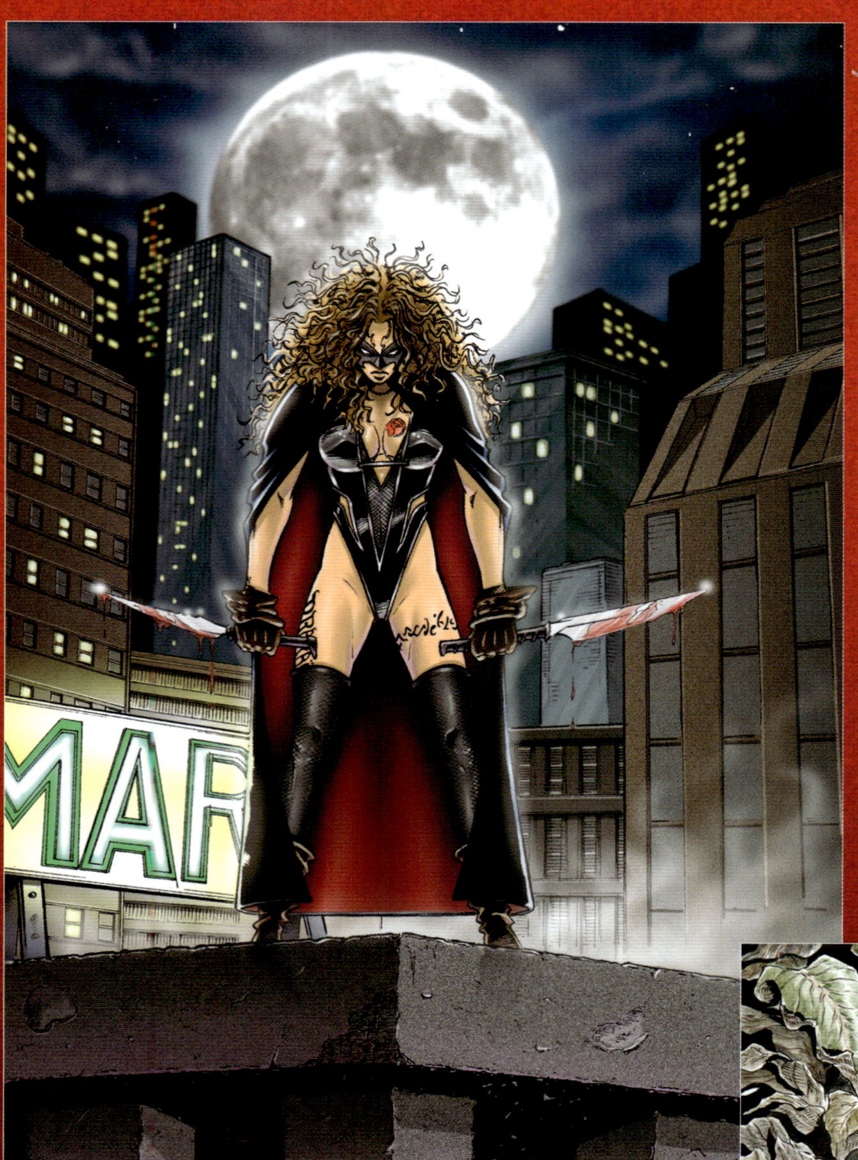

CHRISTOPHE HENIN (France), 2009

Christophe Henin started school in the Sciences before moving to Arts. Product designer, he decided to work in illustration and comics. He works on various projects and comics (such as natalieportman.com and MEDIEVAL CROW) as well as portraits, pin-ups and various visual identity products.

"Drakaina: Dark Heroine"

For this artwork I wanted a darker yet colorful version of Drakaina. Dark in her "Batman-like attitude", yet graphically colorful as you would find in the original comic books.

"Voyage Fantasy"

In this piece I wanted to represent Drakaina in an adventurer's community, guided in her quest by a cute and funny little creature. Drakaina evolves in this virgin land , entering the deep forest, away from the prying eyes of the flying dragons looking for her. My main inspiration for this artwork was "LORD OF THE RINGS - THE COMMUNITY OF THE RING".

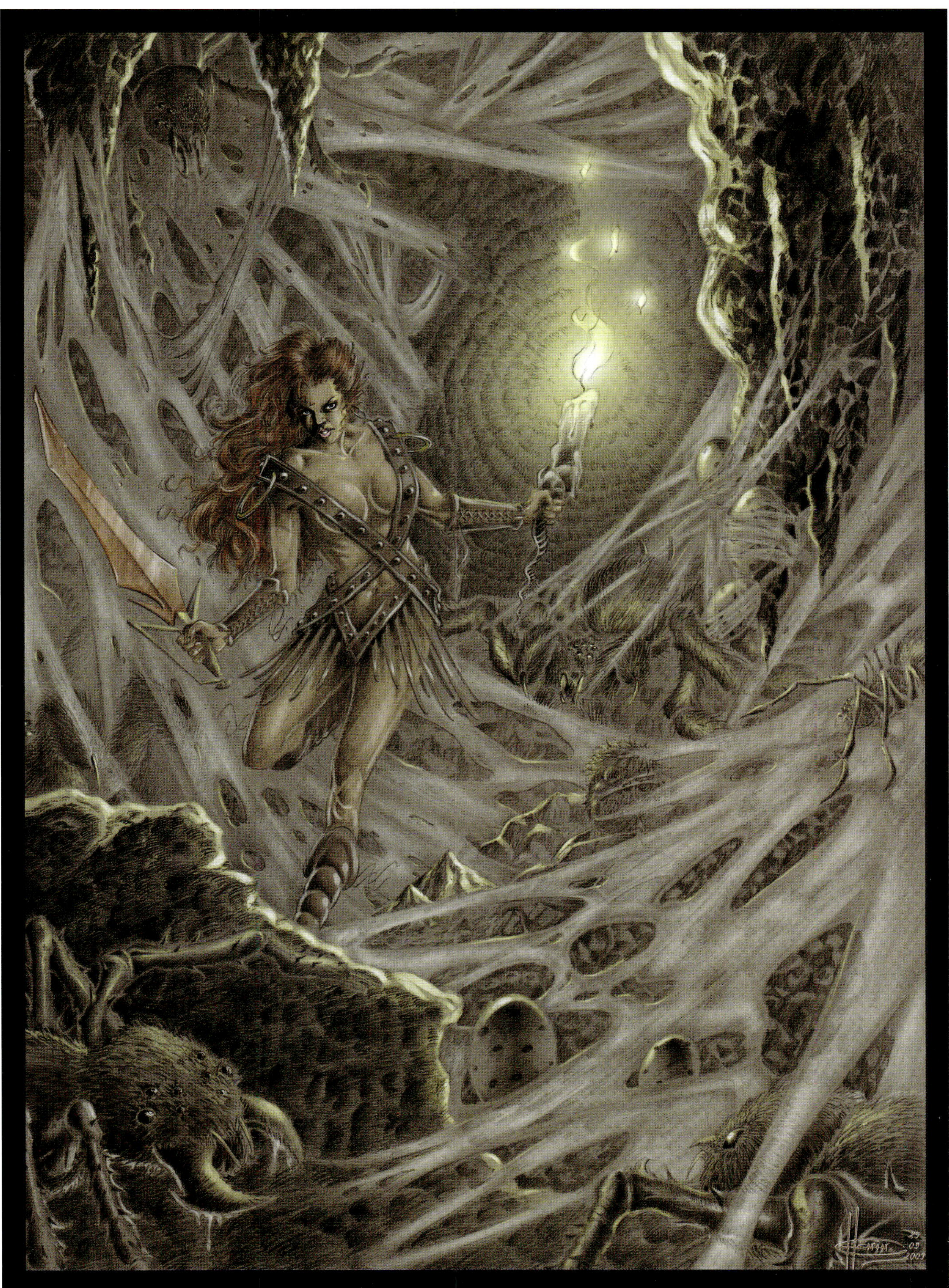

"Spider's Cave"

Once again I drew my inspiration from Peter Jackson's adaptation of Tolkien. Just as Frodo in Shelob's lair, Drakaina walks on a ground filled with gigantic spiders and ants, stared at by the creatures, as they wait for the right moment to take on their prey.

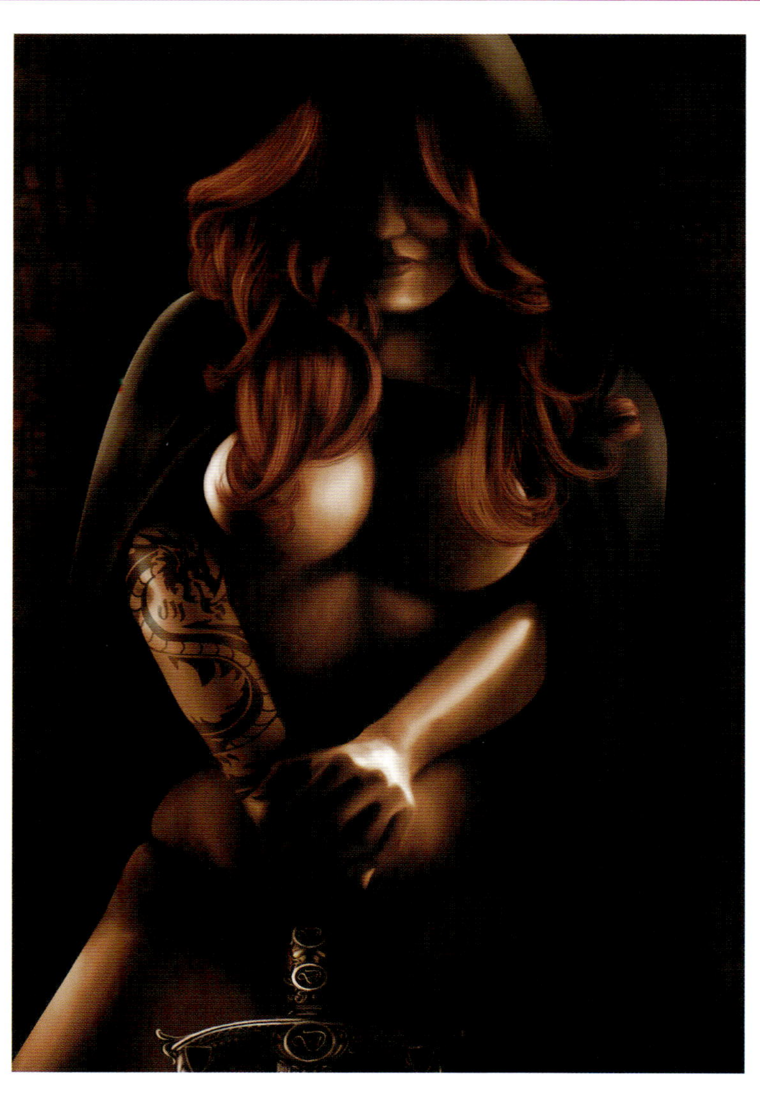

THERREUS (France), 2009

"Heiress of Red Sonja"

The reference picture for this artwork instantly reminded me of Red Sonja. I didn't want to draw yet another Red Sonja, so I thought about making Drakaina her heiress, sexier and darker.

Therreus is a 19 year old French artist with a passion for drawing and CG. His favorite artists are Reinaldo Quintero, Stjepan Sejic and Dan LuVisi.

CHRISTOPHE HENIN (France), 2009

"Drakaina & Tasartir"

After reading Drakaina's biography in another art book, I wanted to portray the deep friendship uniting these two beauties, by pushing their bond to eroticism. The red warrior abandoning herself in the dark amazon's arms.

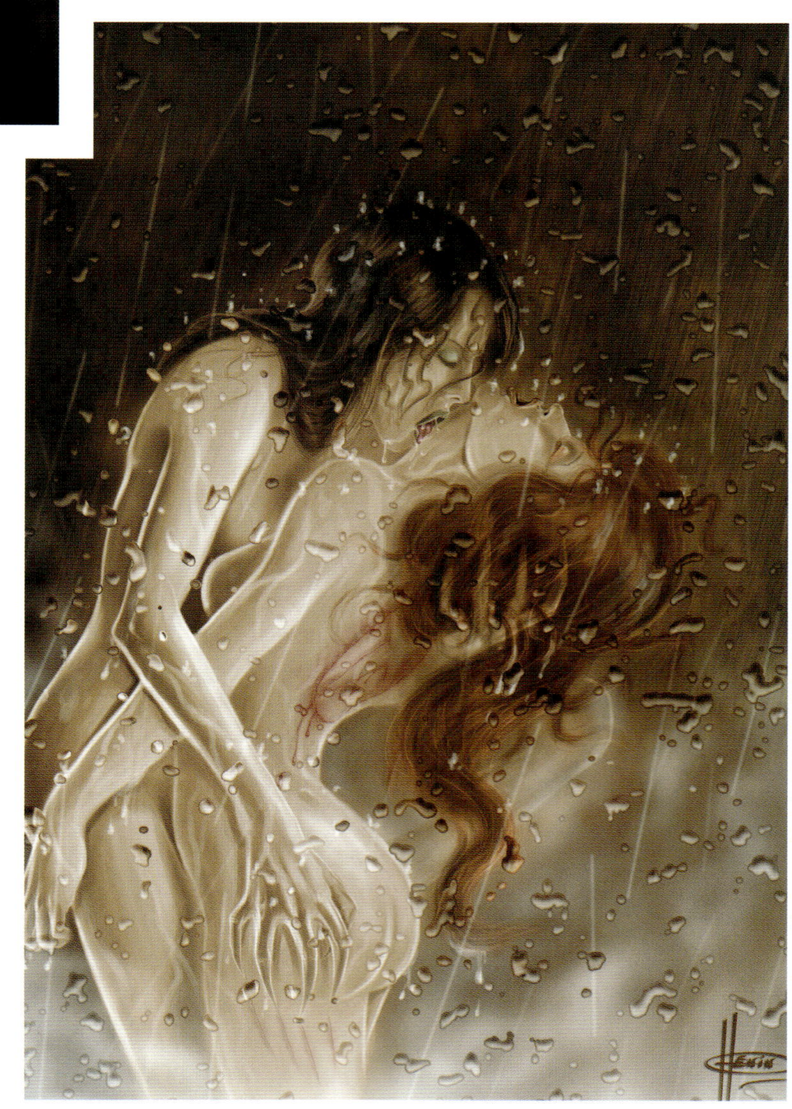

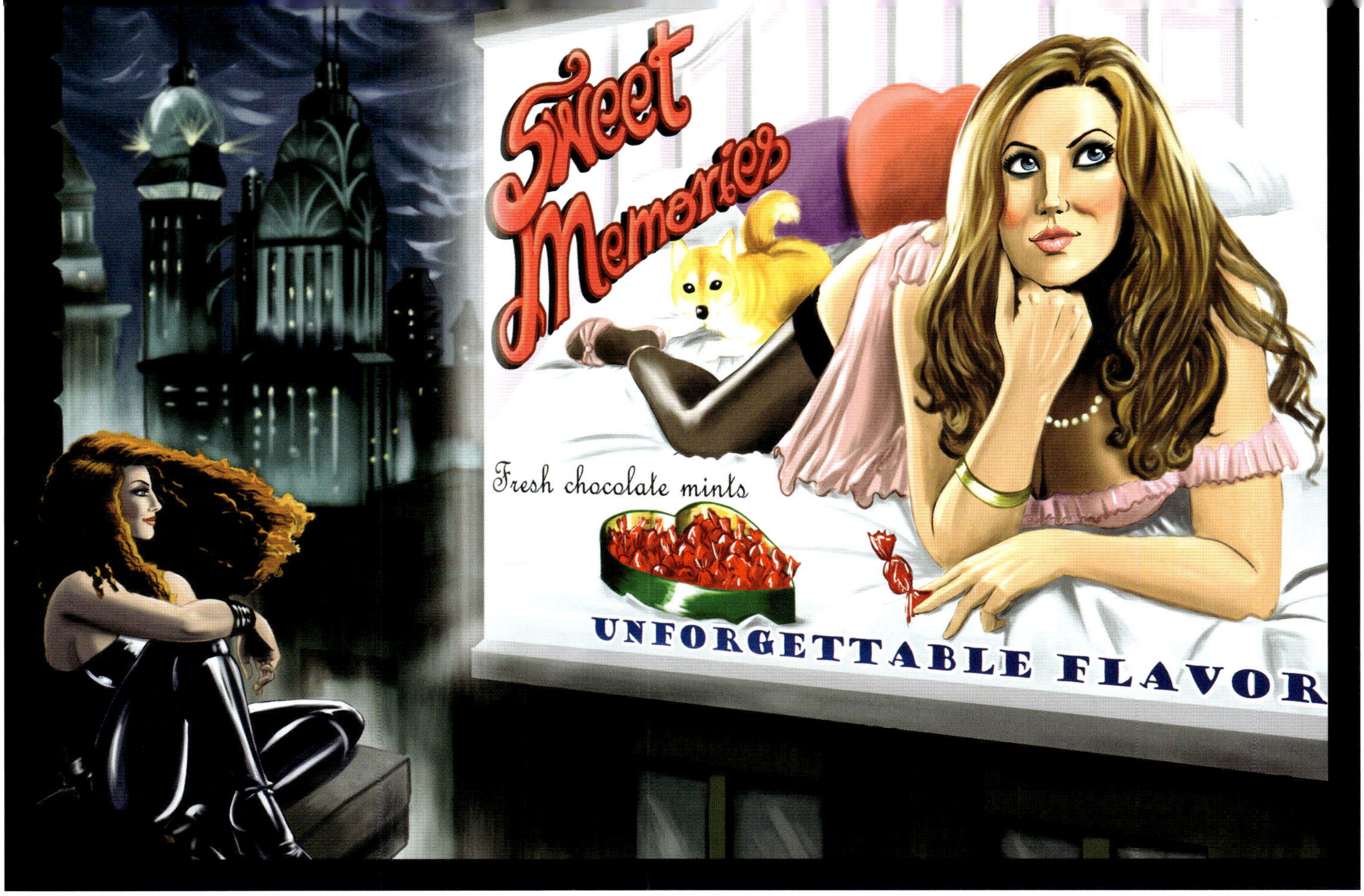

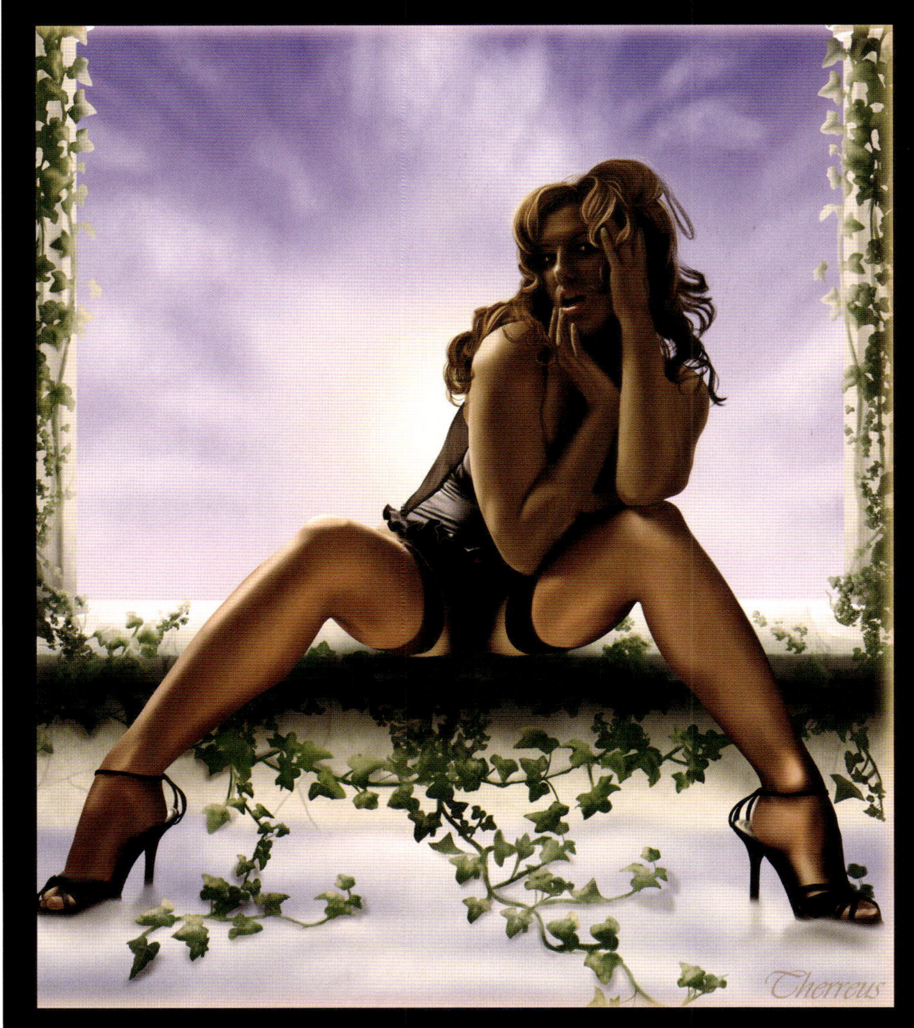

XAVIER MARTI (Spain), 2009
"A Look From Within"

When I did this artwork, I was inspired by the idea of having a double identity. In this case Drakaina portrayed as a pin-up model (with a retro feel) and a nocturnal super-heroine. I also wanted to make a piece which would represent the essence of Drakaina and her duality, so I chose the pin-up and the heroine sides of her. They are two omnipresent traits of her personality and her world of fantasy. I've drawn her with her Shiba Inu because her love for animals and her fight for their rights is also a very important part of her life and message.

THERREUS (France), 2009
"New Age Goddess"
The picture that inspired this painting reminded me of the 'Femme Fatale", incredibly beautiful yet inaccessible, kind of like the Ancient Greek Goddesses. With this painting I wanted to show what a modern Goddess looks like.

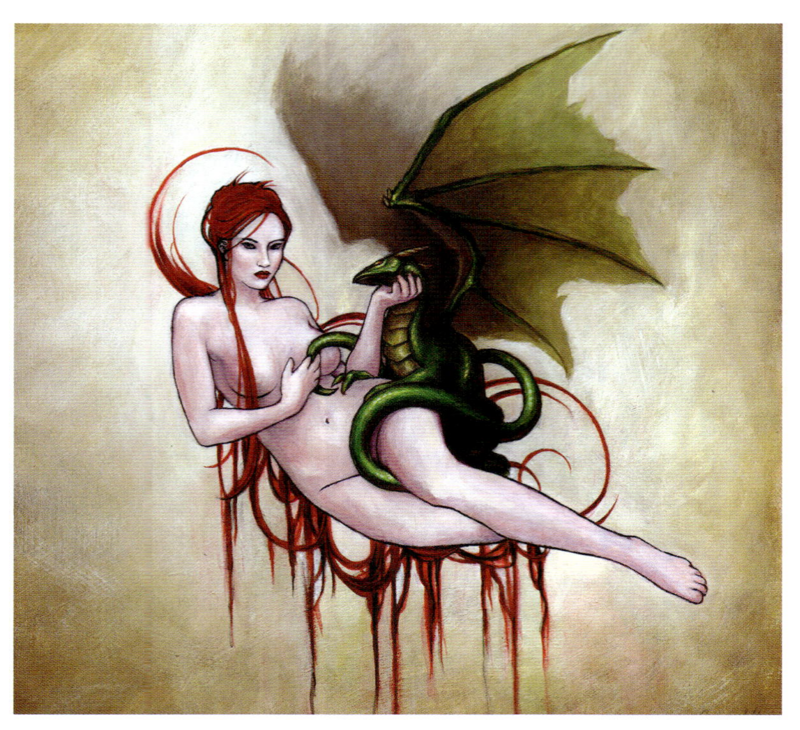

CYNTHIA HALLEY (USA), 2009"
"Drakaina Dragon Queen"

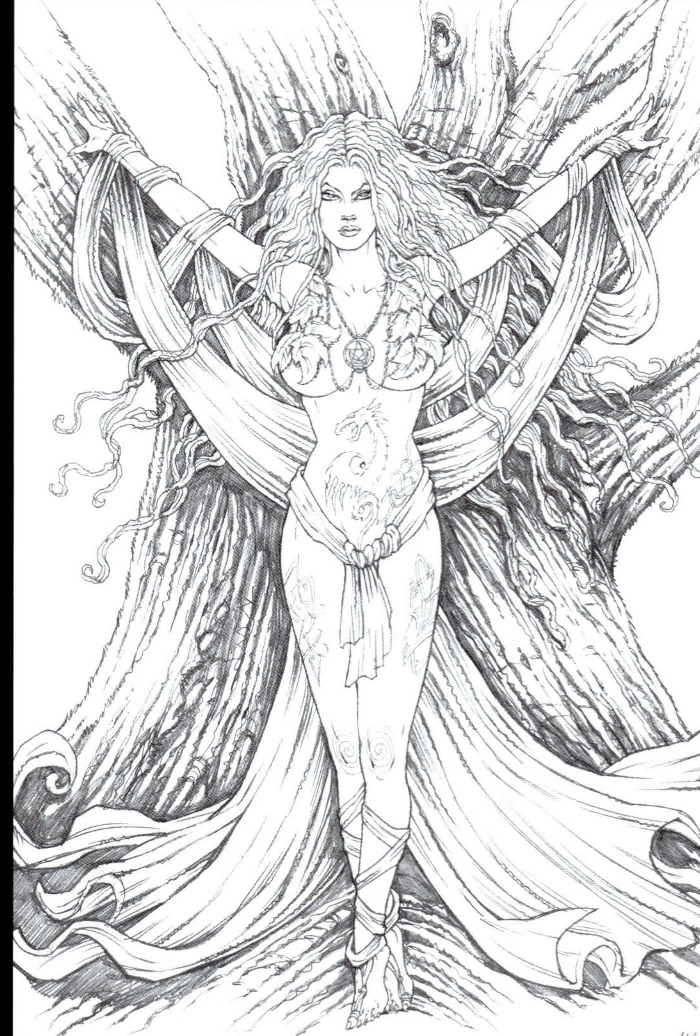

MIKE RATERA (SPAIN), 2008
"Drakaina Wiccan Goddess"

Mike RATERA is a Spanish artist who co-founded the magazine ZERO COMICS in 1981. He has contributed stories to a variety of international comics books.

Mike currently teaches art at the Escola de Comic Joso in Barcelona.

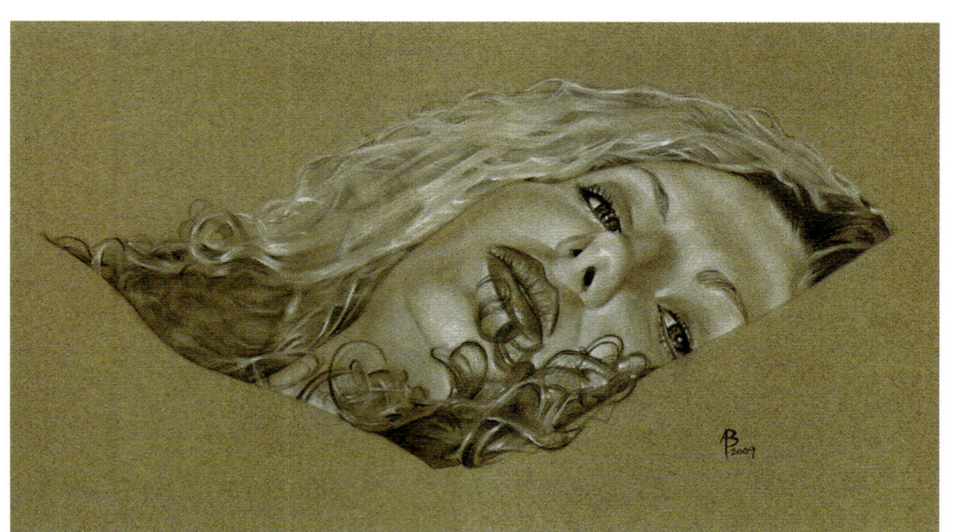

ADAM BRAUM (USA), 2009
Drakaina Drawing
For this drawing, I wanted to capture Drakaina's beauty by focusing on her eyes and framing her face.
Her posture seems relaxed, but the way she is staring at the viewer conveys many different emotions.

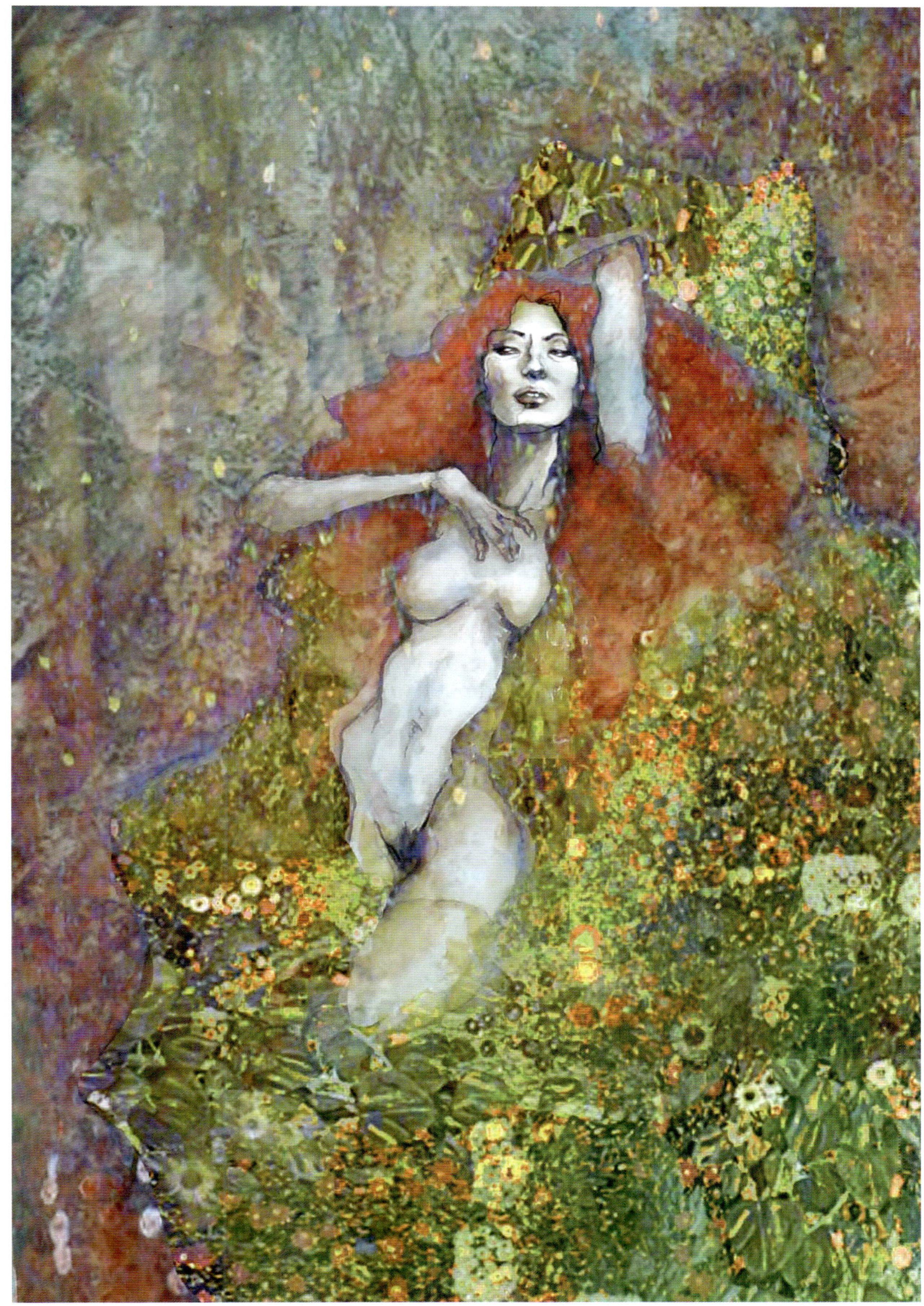

AURORE LEPHILLIPPONAT (France), 2009
"Queen Drakaina"
Freelance illustrator, graphic artist and painter from France, Aurore was only 17 the first time she submitted an artwork to Drakaina, as an entry to a fantasy art competition. Several years later, she has matured a lot and has defined this very particular style of hers.

ARTISTS & PHOTOGRAPHERS IN THIS VOLUME

Adam Braun
www.adambraunart.com

Alexandre Gimbel
www.alexandre-gimbel.blogspot.com

Aurore Lephilipponnat
www.roro33.canalblog.com

Bam Bam
www.bampinups.com

Brian Larter
www.brianlarter.com

Cynthia Halley
www.artaddict.deviantart.com

Christophe Henin
http:perso.wanadoo.fr/christophe.henin.art

Cris Ortega
www.crisortega.com

Daniel Kiessler
www.danielkiessler.com

David Michael Wright
www.davidmichaelwright.com

Didier Normand
www.myspace.com/didiernormand

Edward Reed
www.edwardreed.com

Fabrizio Pasini
www.fabriziopasini.ptibook.com

Fastner and Larson
www.fastnerandlarson.com

Graham Corcoran
www.digitalrampage.com

Johnney W Perkins
www.johnperkinsart.com

Kaze Hine
www.kaze-hime.com

Kelly Futerer
www.kellyx.cghub.com

Lorenzo Di Mauro
www.lorenzodimauro.com

Marco Guaglione
www.marcoguaglione.com

Michael Calandra
www.calandrastudio.com

Mike Ratera
www.mikeratera.blogspot.com

Logan Harding
www.modelmayhem.com/loganharding

Nick Rudnicki
www.nickrudnicki.com

ONEQ
www.myspace.com/oneqkotemufu

Ood Serriere
www.ood-serriere.blogspot.com

Pierluigi Abbondanza
www.abboart.com

Prush
www.blackcenturies.deviantart.com

Renee Biertempfel
www.artbyrenee.com

Rosalys
http://www.rosalys.net

Sandra Chang
www.sandrachang.net

Scarlet Gothica
www.scarletgothica.com

Senyphine (Sandrine Replat)
www.senyphine.com

T.C.COR
www.myspace.com/tccor

Tchals
www.tchals.over-blog.com

Therreus
www.therreus.niloo.fr

Uwe Zarling
www.jarling-arts.com

Xavier Marti
www.xavimarti.com

GETTING IN TOUCH

Want to work with Drakaina and possibly appear in one of her future art books? Or maybe you just want to know more about the one known as the Fantasy Art Muse?? Visit www.drakaina.com for more info.